THE BRITISH HEADCODES

A complete list of all British Railways and London Transport headlamp, disc and two- and four-character codes

M. R. BAILEY

LONDON

Ian Allan Ltd

abc BRITISH RAILWAYS HEADCODES

CONTENTS

Introduction	3
British Railways Headlamp/Disc Codes	5
B.R. Standard	5
Southern Region	7
Cross-London	13
London Midland Region	16
North Eastern Region	20
Four-Character Code	21
First Character	21
Second Character	22
London Midland Region	22
Eastern Region	24
Western Region	28
Special Headcodes	37
Two-Character Codes	37
Southern Region	38
Western Section	38
Central Section	43
Eastern Section	48
Boat trains	55
Freight	55
London Midland Region	59
London Area	59
Western Section	60
Midland Section	60
North Wales Section	61
Lancashire Section	61
Carlisle Section	63
North Eastern Region	63
Teeside	64
Newcastle District	64
Hull and York Districts	64
Wakefield District	65
Leeds District	65
Scottish Region	66
London Transport Executive	66

INTRODUCTION

Many different forms of headcode have been developed over the years on the railways of Britain. The earliest, the standard headlamp classification laid down by the Railway Clearing House, has continued in use right up to the present day but has from time to time and place to place been variously superseded or supplemented by other codes: steam route headcodes, usually discs but lamps at night, used by the southern companies, which later became the Southern Railway, and also on Great Eastern suburban services; electric train headcodes, indicating purely local routes, by position lights on the London Underground, the L.M.S.R. and the L.N.E.R. and by letters (later figures) on the Southern Railway; complementary route and class codes on the Caledonian (semaphore route indicators with normal headlamp class codes); three-figure train numbers, carried by the principal Great Western trains and indicating at first the service and area of origin and later on the service and destination area.

Under the British Railways Modernisation Plan, announced in 1955, the standard locomotive headlamp or disc code was used as first; then a two-character code was evolved for diesel trains, the letter indicating the train class and the figure the route or destination. From all these schemes has been evolved the new British Railways standard four-character code, with a single figure denoting the class, a letter denoting the destination area and a pair of figures denoting either the route or the individual train number. But since not all locomotives are fitted to carry four-figure codes and very few signalboxes yet have the necessary describer apparatus—and since, moreover, some Regions prefer their own code systems, there is a need for a detailed review of what appears at present a somewhat complicated situation.

Descriptions of codes in this book are grouped under three headings: headlamps and discs; four-character; and two-character. The last two sections comprise only descriptions and lists of route numbers; although Class A (1) trains carry individual train numbers, these are far too numerous for inclusion in a book of this size. Each section is prefaced by a short explanation; it is important that this be studied in order that the code lists may be fully understood.

In conclusion, I should like to thank the Publicity and Public Relations Officers of the Regions concerned for their assistance in the preparation of this book.

M.R.B.

Bound for Hastings via Orpington and Battle, six-car diesel-electric unit No. 1033 passes N class 2-6-0 No. 31873 at Petts Wood on a freight for Tonbridge and Ashford.
[D. Cross

BRITISH RAILWAYS HEADLAMP/DISC CODES

In spite of the increasing use of two- and four-character headcodes throughout Britain, headcodes based on the position of headlamps or discs by day and headlamps by night are still the most commonly used system of train identification. Several types are in use: the British standard code; the Southern Region's own white disc and corresponding headlamp code; the inter-regional cross-London freight train code; the London Midland and North Eastern Regions' headcodes; and the London Transport headcode.

B.R. Standard Headlamp/Disc Code

The British standard code is used on all British Railways steam locomotives and diesel shunters and on main line diesel locomotives and diesel multiple-units not yet fitted with panel indicators, except those of the Southern Region and inter-Regional cross-London freight trains.

TRAIN CLASSIFICATION

British Standard Headlamp/Disc Code

Class

- **A**   Express passenger, newspaper, or breakdown train; express diesel car; snow plough on duty; light engine proceeding to assist disabled train.
- **B**   Ordinary passenger, branch passenger or "mixed" train; rail motor (loaded or empty); ordinary passenger or parcels diesel car; breakdown train not on duty.
- **C**   Parcels, fish, fruit, livestock, milk or other perishable train composed entirely of vehicles conforming to coaching stock requirements; express freight, livestock, perishable or ballast train pipe-fitted throughout with the automatic vacuum brake operative on not less than half the vehicles piped to the engine; empty coaching stock (not specially authorised to carry Class A code).
- **D**   Express freight, livestock, perishable or ballast train with not less than one-third vacuum braked vehicles piped to the engine.
- **E**   Express freight, livestock, perishable or ballast train with not less than four vacuum braked vehicles piped to the engine; or express freight of **limited load** not fitted with continuous brake.
- **F**   Express freight, livestock, or ballast train not fitted with continuous brake.
- **G**   Light engine(s) with not more than two brake vans.
- **H**   Through freight or ballast trains not running under C, D, E or F conditions.
- **J**   Mineral or empty wagon train.
- **K**   Pick-up or branch freight, mineral or ballast train.

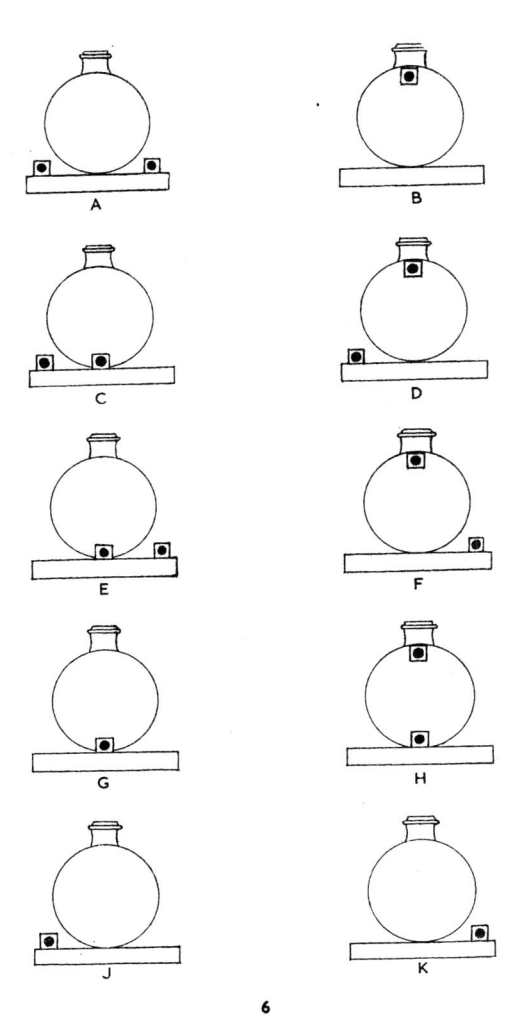

6

Southern Region Locomotive Headlamp/Disc Code

Before the grouping of 1923 many railways had their own individual systems of route identification and perhaps the most spectacular were those of the three Southern groups of companies. On their amalgamation into the Southern Railway, all the different headlamp/disc codes were combined into a standard six-position code, which has been in use ever since.

S.R. Locomotive Headcodes

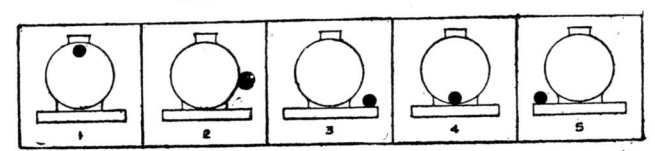

No. 1
  Victoria and Dover via Chatham
  Victoria and Norwood Yard via Selhurst
  Ashford and Hastings
  Reading and Margate via Redhill
  Eastleigh and Bulford via Chandlers Ford and Andover Junction
  Southampton Terminus and Brockenhurst and Weymouth via Wimborne
  Plymouth and Tavistock North
  Woking and Reading via Virginia Water West Curve
  Exeter (Central) and Ilfracombe
  Bodmin and Wadebridge
  Exeter (Central) and Exmouth
  Grateley and Bulford

No. 2
  Victoria or Clapham Junction and Holborn (L.L.)
  London Bridge or Bricklayers' Arms and Portsmouth via Quarry line and Horsham
  Via Mid Kent line and Beckenham Junction
  Ashford and Eastbourne direct
  Waterloo or Nine Elms and Southampton Terminus, direct (not boat trains)
  Willesden and Feltham Yard via Gunnersbury
  Waterloo or Nine Elms and Windsor and Eton (Riverside) via Twickenham
  Yeovil Junction and Yeovil Town
  Seaton Junction and Seaton
  Barnstaple Junction and Torrington
  Halwill and Bude

No. 3
  Victoria or Clapham Junction and Holborn
  London Bridge or Bricklayers' Arms and Brighton via Quarry line
  Tonbridge and Brighton via Eridge

7

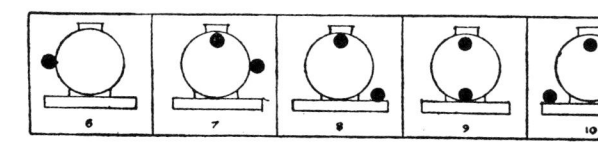

Hastings via Mid Kent line, Oxted, Crowhurst Junction and Tonbridge
Dunton Green and Westerham
Ashford and Margate via Canterbury West
Lydd Branch
Folkestone Junction and Folkestone Harbour
Crowhurst and Bexhill West
Swanley Junction and Gravesend West
Sittingbourne and Sheerness
Deal and Kearsney
Gravesend Central and Allhallows-on-Sea or Grain
All stations to Feltham (except via Mortlake)
Weymouth and Portland and Easton (goods trains)
Bournemouth West and Brockenhurst via Wimborne

No. 4
Victoria or Battersea Yard and Brighton via Redhill
Oxted and Eastbourne via Eridge
London Bridge and New Cross via Bricklayers' Arms Junction
Horsham and Brighton
Bentley and Bordon
Axminster and Lyme Regis
Tipton St. John's and Exmouth
Wareham and Swanage
Brockenhurst and Lymington Pier
Bere Alston and Callington

No. 5
Victoria or Stewarts Lane and Clapham Junction
Oxted and Tunbridge Wells West via East Grinstead (H.L.)
Pulborough and Midhurst
Havant and Hayling Island
London Bridge and Bricklayers' Arms
Tonbridge and Maidstone West
Ashford (Kent) and Dover via Minster and Deal
Stewarts Lane and Victoria
Southampton Docks and Nine Elms via main line (market goods, fruit or potato train)

No. 6
London Bridge or Bricklayers' Arms and Dover or Ramsgate via East Croydon, Oxted and Tonbridge
Battersea Yard and Kensington (Olympia)
Waterloo or Nine Elms and Reading South via Twickenham
Willesden and Feltham Yard via Kew East Junction
Exeter Central and Sidmouth
Eastleigh or Southampton and Fawley
Bournemouth Central and Brockenhurst via Wimborne
Torrington and Halwill
Three Bridges and Tunbridge Wells West

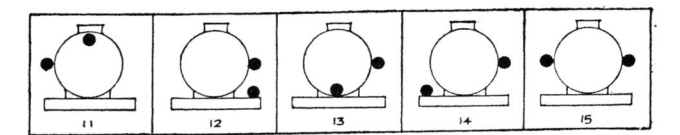

No. 7
　　Victoria or Battersea Yard and Portsmouth Harbour via Quarry line and Horsham
　　Via Maidstone East line to Victoria or Holborn Viaduct
　　Waterloo or Nine Elms and Southampton Docks via Brentford Central, Chertsey and Woking

No. 8
　　London Bridge or Bricklayers' Arms and Eastbourne or Hastings via Quarry line
　　Victoria or West London Line and Ramsgate via Herne Hill or Catford Loop
　　London Bridge or Bricklayers' Arms and Hastings via Chislehurst and Tunbridge Wells Central
　　West London line to East Croydon via Crystal Palace
　　Special boat trains Waterloo and Southampton Docks via Northam
　　Special boat trains from Southampton Docks to Waterloo via Millbrook
　　Southampton and Andover Junction via Redbridge
　　Feltham Yard and Brent via Kew East Junction

No. 9
　　Victoria or Battersea Yard and Eastbourne or Hastings via Quarry Line
　　London and Hither Green Sidings
　　Victoria and Folkestone Harbour or Dover Marine via Swanley, Otford and Tonbridge
　　Waterloo or Nine Elms and Plymouth
　　Bournemouth Central and Dorchester South goods trains
　　Battersea Yard and Brent via New Kew Junction
　　Southampton Terminus and Portsmouth Harbour via Netley

No. 10
　　London Bridge or Bricklayers' Arms and Portsmouth via Redhill and Horsham
　　Victoria or Battersea Yard and Norwood Yard via Crystal Palace
　　London Bridge and New Cross Gate to Eardley Sidings via Peckham Rye
　　Deptford Wharf and New Cross Gate
　　London Bridge or Bricklayers' Arms and Folkestone or Dover via Chislehurst, Tonbridge and Ashford
　　Dover and Margate via Deal
　　Special boat trains Waterloo to Southampton Docks via Millbrook
　　Feltham to Durnsford Road via Chertsey

No. 11
　　Victoria or Battersea Yard and Portsmouth via Redhill and Horsham
　　Via Dartford Loop line
　　Victoria or Holborn Viaduct and Hastings via Orpington and Tunbridge Wells Central
　　Waterloo or Nine Elms and Southampton Terminus via Alton
　　Salisbury and Bournemouth West via Wimborne

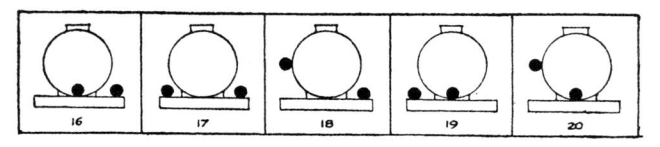

Fareham and Gosport
Ballast trains to Meldon Quarry from Exeter Central and stations West thereof

No. 12
Victoria or Battersea Yard and Portsmouth Harbour via Mitcham Junction
London Bridge or Bricklayers' Arms and Eastbourne or Hastings via Redhill
Victoria, Stewarts Lane or Holborn Viaduct to North Kent line via Nunhead line
Nine Elms and Feltham via Mortlake
Down main line goods terminating at Woking
Southampton Docks and Salisbury via Eastleigh

No. 13
London Bridge or Bricklayers' Arms and Brighton via Redhill
West London line to Northwood Yard via Thornton Heath
Victoria or Holborn Viaduct to Dover via Nunhead line and Maidstone East
Parcels and empty trains Waterloo to Clapham Junction (Kensington sidings)
Feltham Yard and Neasden via Kew East Junction
Portsmouth Harbour or Portsmouth and Southsea to Fratton
Exeter Central and Exmouth Junction
Bournemouth West to Dorchester South
Southampton and Salisbury via Redbridge

No. 14
London Bridge, Oxted and Tunbridge Wells West via Hever
London Bridge or Bricklayers' Arms and Dover via Chislehurst Loop and Maidstone East
Waterloo or Nine Elms and Brockenhurst and Bournemouth West via Sway

No. 15
Via Bexleyheath Line
Victoria, Stewarts Lane or Holborn via Nunhead Line and Bexleyheath
Waterloo or Nine Elms and Reading South via loop line
All trains terminating at Portsmouth and Southsea (trains from Salisbury to carry No. 17 to Eastleigh)
Exeter Central and Padstow
Light engines, Bournemouth Central or Bournemouth West to Bournemouth Central via triangle to turn
Light engines Eastleigh Loco. to Portsmouth and Southsea
Light engines to Guildford Loco. via Woking (except via Staines Central)
Clapham Junction and Kensington (Olympia)

No. 16
London Bridge or Bricklayers' Arms and Portsmouth via West Croydon
Victoria or Battersea Yard and Eastbourne or Hastings via Redhill
London Bridge or Bricklayers' Arms and Ramsgate via Tonbridge and Canterbury West
Waterloo or Nine Elms and Woking via Richmond and Chertsey
Milk and empty trains to Clapham Junction via Byfleet curve and Richmond

| 21 | 22 | 23 | 24 | 25 |

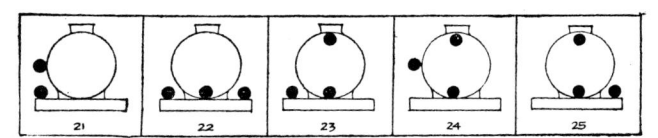

No. 17
    London Bridge or Bricklayers' Arms and Tonbridge or Reading South via East Croydon and Redhill (also Tonbridge and Reading)
    Brighton and Hove via Preston Park Spur
    Three Bridges and Eridge
    Victoria or Holborn and Folkestone or Dover via Orpington, Tonbridge and Ashford
    Victoria or Battersea Yard and Portsmouth Harbour via Thornton Heath, West Croydon and Horsham
    London Bridge or Bricklayers' Arms and Gillingham, Faversham, Ramsgate or Dover via Chislehurst and Chatham
    Waterloo or Nine Elms and Clapham Junction (empty trains and light engines)
    Passenger trains Bournemouth Central and Weymouth

No. 18
    London Bridge or Bricklayers' Arms and Dover, Ramsgate or Hastings via Chislehurst, Swanley, Otford and Sevenoaks
    Victoria, Oxted and Tunbridge Wells West via Edenbridge Town
    Holborn and Ramsgate via Herne Hill or Catford Loop
    Light engines and trains requiring to run to up main loop, Clapham Junction, from stations westward
    Southampton and Andover Junction via Eastleigh

No. 19
    Victoria or Battersea Yard and Brighton via Quarry line
    London Bridge or New Cross Gate and Norwood Yard
    Tunbridge Wells West and Eastbourne
    Victoria or Holborn Viaduct and Ramsgate, Dover or Hastings via Nunhead line and Tonbridge
    Horsham and Guildford
    Twickenham and Shepperton
    Waterloo or Nine Elms and Exeter Central via East Putney
    Salisbury and Portsmouth Harbour via Eastleigh
    Portsmouth and Southsea to Salisbury via Eastleigh
    Light engines or engines with vehicles attached running round the triangle at Bournemouth West to turn

No. 20
    Victoria, Stewarts Lane or Holborn to Ramsgate via Nunhead line, Chislehurst and Chatham
    London Bridge or Bricklayers' Arms and North Kent line via Greenwich
    Via Streatham Spur
    Salisbury and Portsmouth Harbour via Redbridge

No. 21
    Victoria and Newhaven Harbour
    Victoria or Holborn Viaduct to Ramsgate via Nunhead line and Maidstone East
    Waterloo or Nine Elms and Portsmouth Harbour via Woking and Guildford
    Light engines from all stations to Feltham Loco.
    Light engines from all stations west of Basingstoke to Eastleigh Loco.

| 26 | 27 | 28 | 29 | 30 |

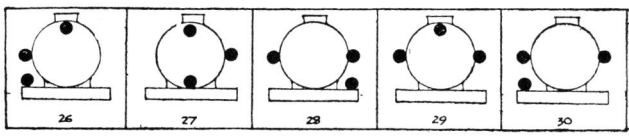

No. 22
  Waterloo and Portsmouth Harbour via Eastleigh
  Feltham and Brent via Richmond
  S.R. and W.R. trains Hither Green Sidings, Stewarts Lane or South Lambeth to Old Oak Common
  L.M. (Western Division) trains between Willesden and Redhill via Clapham Junction
  L.M. (Midland Division) and E.R. (G.N.) trains to or from Hither Green Sidings
  W.R. trains, Norwood Yard to Old Oak Common

No. 23
  Nine Elms and Willesden via New Kew Junction
  Brighton and Salisbury via Southampton Central
  Eastleigh and Micheldever or Basingstoke (light engines for testing)
  Windsor and Eton Riverside and Redhill via Guildford
  W.R. trains to South Lambeth
  E.R. trains to or from Lower Sydenham

No. 24
  Waterloo and Guildford via Leatherhead
  Southampton and Willesden via Richmond and Gunnersbury
  Southampton or Salisbury and Willesden via Chertsey and Kew East Junction (or from Basingstoke)
  Reading South to Willesden via Feltham

No. 25
  Nine Elms and Brent via New Kew Junction
  Brighton and Salisbury through trains via Eastleigh
  To L.M.R. via West London line

No. 26
  Brighton and Bournemouth
  Victoria (E. or C.), Stewarts Lane, Clapham Junction or Holborn and Eardley Sidings via Herne Hill

No. 27
  Hither Green Sidings and Feltham via Brentford Central
  Feltham to Wimbledon West Yard via Chertsey
  London Bridge or Bricklayers' Arms and Brighton via Oxted, Eridge and Lewes

No. 28
  Hither Green Sidings and Feltham via Richmond

No. 29
  Waterloo and Lymington Pier
  Plumstead and Feltham via Brentford Central
  Victoria or Battersea Yard and Brighton via Edenbridge Town, Eridge and Lewes

No. 30
  Plumstead and Feltham via Richmond
  Waterloo and Weymouth via Ringwood

Cross-London Headlamp/Disc Code

So extensive is the freight traffic across London and so numerous the reception goods sidings that a special code is used to distinguish the many different destination points. For simplicity's sake, some code numbers are repeated for several goods yards at some distance from each other. In all cases (except where otherwise stated) the illustrations represent lighted lamps by night and either white discs or lighted lamps throughout the day. The B.R. standard four-character code will supersede the headlamp code when all the locomotives concerned have been fitted with indicator panels. The Southern Region has introduced its own two-character code for its diesel–hauled freights (see page 55).

Ref. No.	Route
1	Earls Court or Kensington and Willesden Eastern Region and Moorgate
2	Brent and Kensington High Street (by night only) Eastern Region and New Cross Gate
3	Midland lines or Eastern Region and Clapham Junction via Blackfriars Junction Midland lines or Eastern Region and Victoria Midland lines or Eastern Region and Battersea Yard via Blackfriars Junction Liverpool Street and Whitechapel Sidings
4	Willesden to Shepherds Bush Brent and Herne Hill via Barnes
5	Willesden and Hither Green Brent to Battersea via New Kew Junction Western Region to Smithfield or Farringdon Liverpool Street or Whitechapel Sidings and New Cross or New Cross Gate
6	Willesden and Clapham Junction, Norwood and East Croydon, or Clapham Junction and Victoria
7	Willesden and South Lambeth Midland lines E.C.S. to or from Moorgate Freight trains to or from Bow Depot via South Tottenham and Stratford
8	Willesden and Kensington coal yard or Lillie Bridge All trains to Willesden Junction via West London and West London Extension lines Willesden or Old Kew Junction and Acton (L.M.R.) Hammersmith and Kew Bridge (freight and milk trains and light engines) Midland passenger trains to or from Moorgate Brent and Hammersmith or Kew Bridge (by night only)
9	All trains to Chelsea Dock Freight trains between St. Pancras and Poplar via South Tottenham Brent and Hither Green via Barnes, Factory Junction and Nunhead
10	Willesden and Stewarts Lane, Blackfriars or Holborn, and between Holborn, Blackfriars and Cannon Street Midland lines to or from Cannon Street

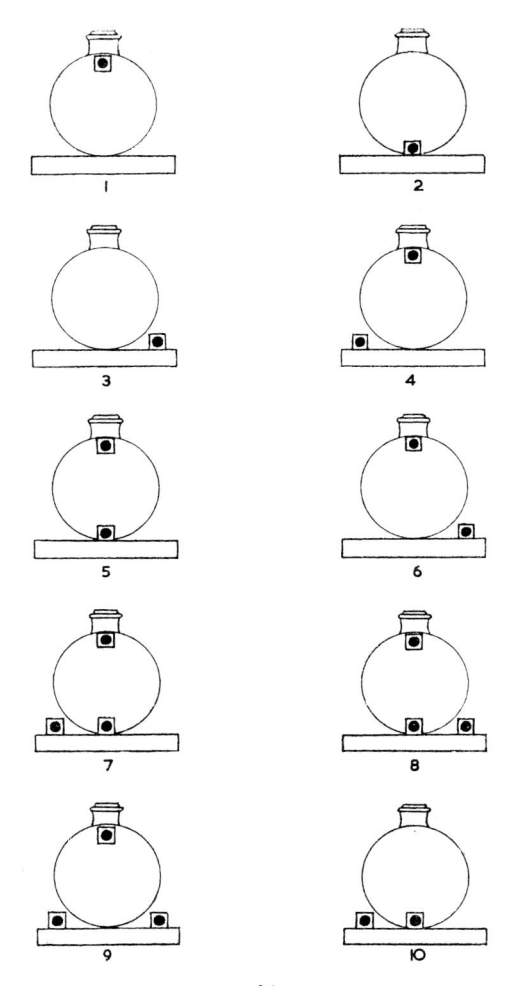

14

11	12
13	14
15	16
17	18
19	

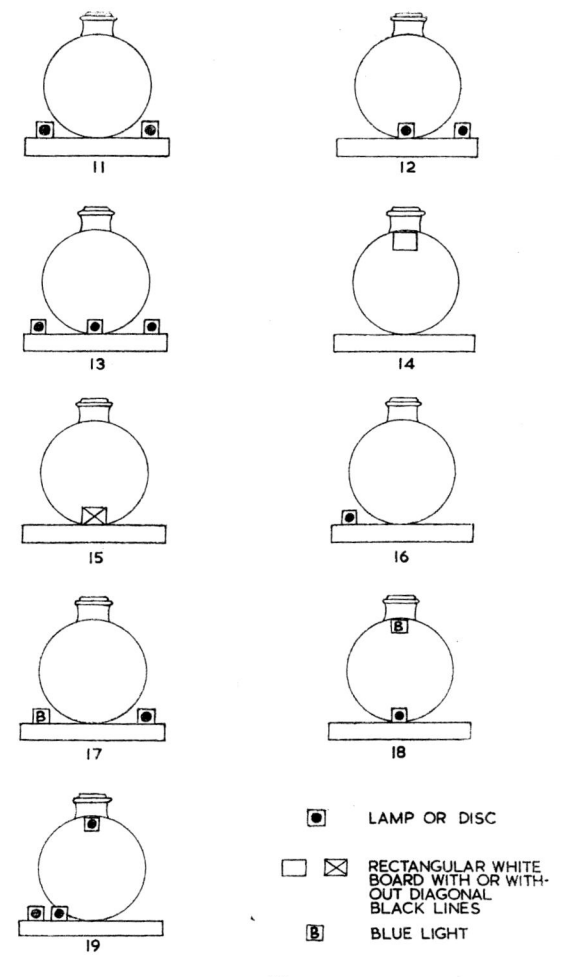

- ● LAMP OR DISC
- □ ⊠ RECTANGULAR WHITE BOARD WITH OR WITHOUT DIAGONAL BLACK LINES
- B BLUE LIGHT

Ref. No.	Route
	Brent and Acton (W.R.) W.R. goods to and from Smithfield
11	Midland lines or Eastern Region and Bricklayers' Arms
12	All trains to Brompton and Fulham Brent and West Kensington (by night only) Midland lines to or from Walworth coal sidings Midland lines to or from Herne Hill sorting sidings Willesden and Norwood or East Croydon Brent and Hammersmith or Kew Bridge (by day only)
13	All trains to Falcon Lane Midland lines or the Eastern Region and Hither Green Willesden and Redhill via Clapham Junction
14	Brent and Kensington High Street (by day only)
15	Brent and West Kensington (by day only)
16	Eastern Region Goods to Farringdon Depot Liverpool Street or Whitechapel Sidings and Hither Green Sidings
17	Moorgate and South Tottenham line
18	London Midland Region to Moorgate Moorgate to Hendon
19	L.T.E. train; Neasden and Hammersmith

London Midland Region Headlamp Code

Before the Crewe-Manchester electrification in 1960, the only electrified lines on the L.M.R. were the Lancashire (Wirral and Mersey, Liverpool-Southport, Lancaster, Morecambe & Heysham, Manchester-Altrincham, Manchester-Glossop-Hadfield and Manchester-Bury) and London (Broad Street-Richmond and Euston-Watford) suburban lines. All used the same four-aspect headlamp code; but the new stock in the London area and on the Manchester-Bury line use two- and four-character codes respectively.

L.M.R. Headlamp Code

London Area (still used by the few remaining L.M.S. sets)

Ref. No.	Route
1	To Euston and Watford, except from Broad Street; and Broad Street and Willesden via Hampstead Junction line
2	Broad Street and Watford
3	Broad Street and Willesden to Richmond
4	To Croxley Green
5	To Harrow
6	To Willesden (New Station)
7	To Bushey
8	Empty trains to Mitre shed
9	Empty trains to Euston
10	Empty trains to Broad Street

HEADLIGHT OBSCURED ●

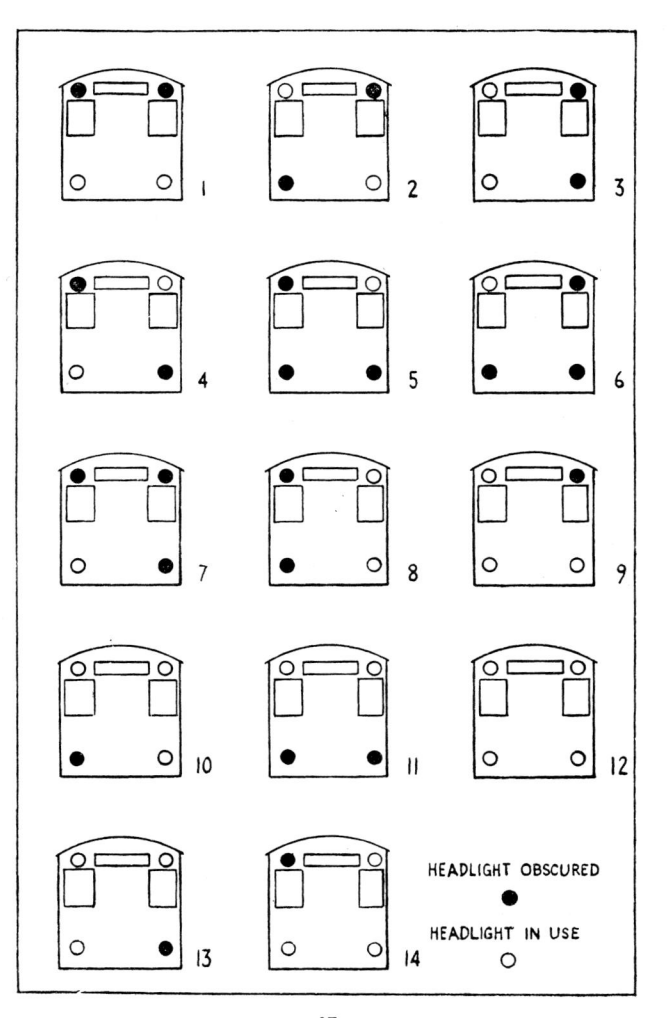

HEADLIGHT IN USE ○

OIL LAMP

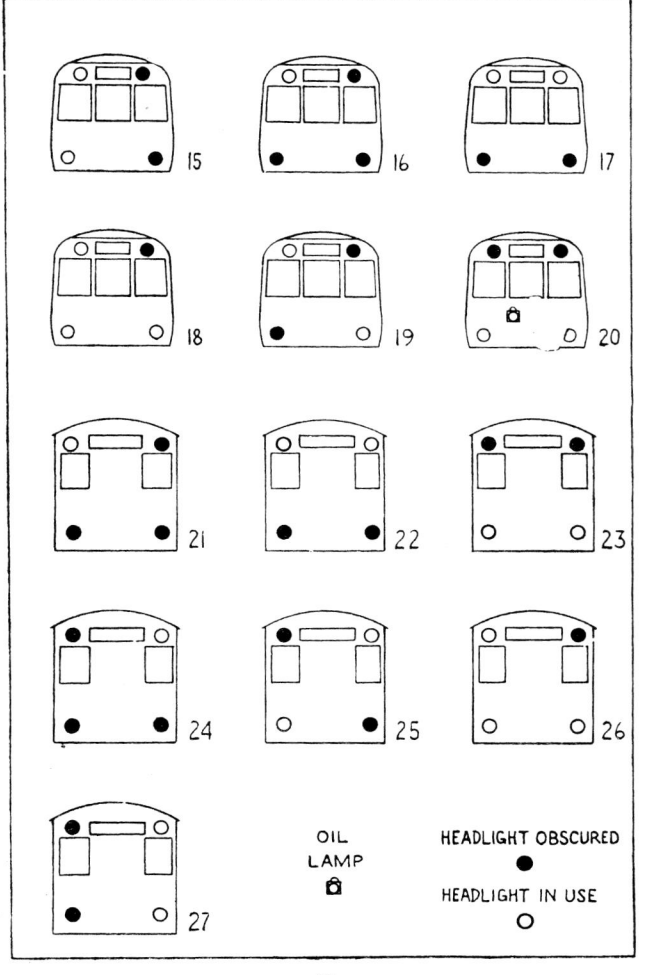

HEADLIGHT OBSCURED ●

HEADLIGHT IN USE ○

Ref. No.	Route
11	Empty trains to Harrow
12	Empty trains to Croxley shed
13	Empty trains to Stonebridge Park shed
14	Empty trains to Watford

Wirral and Mersey lines

15	Liverpool Central (L.L.) and West Kirby; Birkenhead (North) to Liverpool Central (L.L.)
16	Liverpool Central (L.L.) and New Brighton; Liverpool (Central) (L.L.) and Birkenhead Park; New Brighton and Birkenhead Park
17	Liverpool Central (L.L.) and Rock Ferry
18	Empty trains between West Kirby and Birkenhead (North) and Birkenhead (North) to Birkenhead Park
19	Empty trains between Birkenhead Park and New Brighton

Liverpool-Southport line

20	All loaded, empty and baggage trains for all destinations

Lancaster, Morecambe and Heysham line

21	Loaded trains for all destinations
22	Empty trains for all destinations

Manchester-Altrincham line

23	Express or non-stop
24	All stations
25	Empty trains
26	Express or non-stop terminating other than Altrincham or Manchester (Oxford Road)
27	All stations terminating other than Altrincham or Manchester (Oxford Road)

Manchester-Glossop-Hadfield line

28	Manchester (Piccadilly) and Hadfield direct
29	Manchester (Piccadilly) and Glossop or Hadfield via Glossop
30	Staff train, Ashburys and Mottram Yard Halt
31	Empty trains

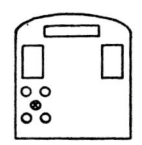

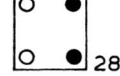

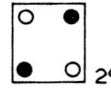

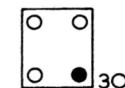

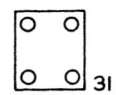

● HEADLIGHT OBSCURED ○ HEADLIGHT IN USE ⊗ RED TAIL-LIGHT

North Eastern Region Headlamp Code

When the B.R. standard electric stock was introduced in 1955 on the North and South Tyneside suburban services, the original headlamp code was retained. The position of the groups of lights was, however, changed to conform with the design. The lights on the original stock still in service are grouped below the right-hand window of the driver's cab while those on the B.R. stock have a central position.

N.E.R. Headlamp Code

Ref. No.   **Route**

1. Newcastle (Central), Tynemouth and Manors North via Riverside
2. Newcastle (Central), Tynemouth, Monkseaton and Manors North via Heaton
3. Newcastle (Central), Tynemouth and Monkseaton via Benton and south-east curve
4. Newcastle (Central) and Manors North via Benton and south-west curve
5. Newcastle (Central), Manors North, South Gosforth and Monkseaton
6. Gosforth car sheds or Newcastle (Central) to South Shields, South Shields to Newcastle (Central)
7. Empty trains to Newcastle (Central) or Gosforth car sheds

NORTH EASTERN REGION HEADCODE

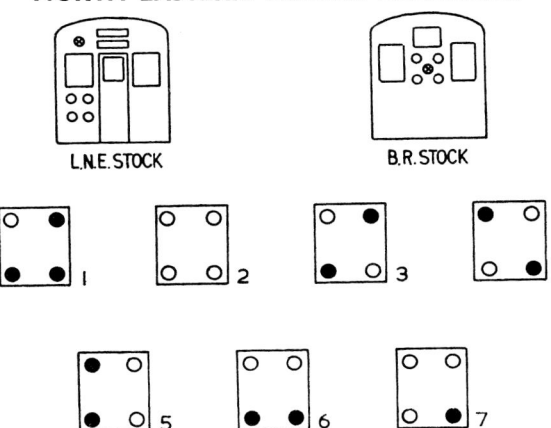

L.N.E. STOCK   B.R. STOCK

● HEADLIGHT OBSCURED   ○ HEADLIGHT IN USE   ⊗ RED TAIL-LIGHT

BRITISH RAILWAYS STANDARD FOUR-CHARACTER HEADCODE

Improved signalling methods and the resultant increase in track occupation made it necessary to evolve a more accurate and positive system of train identification. It was decided under the Modernisation Plan that the standard headcode should incorporate the train classification, destination and route or train number (if any) in a single code, a system similar to that which had been used for some years by the Western Region. The original Western Region code used three characters for train identification only; the class was displayed by the standard headlamp code. Recently, however, the Western Region evolved a new four-character code of which the first two characters gave the classification and destination area and the last two the train number. This code has been adopted as the standard for British Railways but instead of using a number for the destination area, in the second position, a letter has been used to allow a much greater number of areas to be coded. Where traffic is too dense for individual train numbers to be used route numbers are substituted and these are listed under Regional headings below.

Before the introduction of the four-character standard code, two-character codes were used, details of which appear in the section beginning on page 37. These codes are still widely used on stock which has not yet been fitted with a four-character panel. Some Regions are retaining their two-character code; or displaying it in the last two positions of the standard four-character panel, leaving the first two positions blank. Where this is done, a white bar is displayed above the number.

The new four-character code will eventually be used throughout the London Midland, Western and Eastern Regions. Locomotives and multiple-units at present fitted to carry two-character or headlamp codes are being modified to carry the four-character code as they become due for overhaul.

First Character

This code number indicates the train class and replaces the corresponding lamp/disc code (see page 5).

New Code	Original Classification
1	A
2	B
3	C
4	C

New Code	Original Classification
5	D
6	E
7	F
8	H
9	J and K
0	G

Second Character

The code letter which occupies the second position indicates the train's destination area. Each Region has its own group of letters, listed separately on succeeding pages. For Inter-Regional trains a universal code is in force:

Code	Destination
E	Eastern Region
M	London Midland Region
N	North Eastern Region
O	Southern Region
S	Scottish Region
V	Western Region
X	Excursion and special trains

London Midland Region

The four-character code is as yet used only in the Liverpool and Manchester areas of the London Midland Region. In other areas where the two-character code is still used, the four-character code is being introduced as it becomes possible to modify stock.

REGIONAL AREA CODE

Code	Destination Area
A	Euston lines
B	Euston and Rugby lines
C	St. Pancras and Marylebone lines
D	Nottingham and Chester area
F	Leicester area
G	Birmingham area (Western and Midland lines)
H	South Manchester and Stoke areas
J	North Manchester area
K	Liverpool (Lime Street) and (Central), and Crewe areas
L	Barrow, Preston (excluding Fylde) and Carlisle areas
P	Blackpool, Fylde and Derby areas
T	Excursion and special trains local to L.M.R., or on freight trains indicating a trip train
Z	Special code used for particular trains (See page 37)

THIRD AND FOURTH CHARACTERS

Individual train numbers run from 00 to 99. Where a series of train numbers exceeds 99, the numbers recommence at 00; it is stipulated that at least 12 hours must elapse between two trains of the same number. Parcels trains in each area carry train numbers from 00 to 29; Inter-district E.C.S. trains not for traffic 30 to 49; and freight trains conforming to the new code have a separate list of numbers from 00 to 99 in each area. Passenger train routes are numbered 50 to 99; those so far introduced are:

Code	Route
50	Alderley Edge and Stockport
	Wigan and Liverpool (Lime Street)
51	Alderley Edge and Manchester (Oxford Road) via Styal
	St. Helens and Liverpool (Lime Street)
52	Alderley Edge and Manchester (Oxford Road) via Stockport
	Manchester (Exchange) and Liverpool (Lime Street) via Patricroft
53	Alderley Edge and Manchester (Piccadilly) via Styal
	Manchester (Exchange) and Liverpool (Lime Street) via Tyldesley
54	Alderley Edge and Manchester (Piccadilly) via Stockport
	Newton-le-Willows or Earlstown and Liverpool (Lime Street)
55	Wilmslow and Manchester (Oxford Road) via Styal
	Manchester (Exchange) and Earlstown via Patricroft
56	Wilmslow and Manchester (Oxford Road) via Stockport
	Manchester (Exchange) and St. Helens via Patricroft
57	Wilmslow and Manchester (Piccadilly) via Styal
	Warrington (Bank Quay) and Wigan (North Western)
58	Wilmslow and Manchester (Piccadilly) via Stockport
	Warrington (Bank Quay) and Earlstown
59	Stockport and Manchester (Piccadilly)
	Warrington (Bank Quay) and St. Helens
60	Stockport and Manchester (Oxford Road)
	Earlstown and St. Helens
61	Crewe or Chelford and Manchester (Piccadilly) via Styal
	St. Helens Junction and St. Helens
62	Crewe or Chelford and Manchester (Piccadilly) via Stockport
63	Crewe or Chelford and Manchester (Oxford Road) via Styal
64	Crewe or Chelford and Manchester (Oxford Road) via Stockport
65	Uttoxeter or Cresswell and Manchester (Piccadilly) via Stoke-on-Trent and Cheadle Hulme
66	Uttoxeter or Cresswell and Manchester (Oxford Road) via Stoke-on-Trent and Cheadle Hulme
67	Birmingham, Stafford, Stoke-on-Trent or Congleton and Manchester (Piccadilly) via Cheadle Hulme
68	Birmingham, Stafford, Stoke-on-Trent or Congleton and Manchester (Oxford Road) via Cheadle Hulme
69	Macclesfield and Manchester (Piccadilly) via Cheadle Hulme
	Holyhead or Bangor and Liverpool (Lime Street)
70	Macclesfield and Manchester (Oxford Road) via Cheadle Hulme
	Llandudno and Liverpool (Lime Street)
	Leigh and Manchester (Exchange) via Tyldesley
71	Buxton line and Manchester (Piccadilly)
	Chester or Helsby and Liverpool (Lime Street)
	Leigh and Tyldesley only
72	Buxton line and Manchester (Oxford Road)
	Birkenhead (West) and Liverpool (Lime Street)
	Kenyon Junction and Manchester (Exchange) via Patricroft
73	Macclesfield or Rose Hill and Manchester (Piccadilly) via Belle Vue and Ardwick Junction
	Crewe or Stoke-on-Trent and Liverpool (Lime Street)
74	Macclesfield or Rose Hill and Manchester (Piccadilly) via Hyde Junction and Ardwick Junction
	Runcorn or Ditton Junction and Liverpool (Lime Street)

Code	Route
75	Hayfield, New Mills or Marple and Manchester (Piccadilly) via Belle Vue and Ardwick Junction
	Manchester (Oxford Road) and Liverpool (Lime Street)
76	Hayfield, New Mills or Marple and Manchester (Piccadilly) via Hyde Junction and Ardwick Junction
	Warrington (Bank Quay) and Liverpool (Lime Street)
77	Eastern Region via Dunford Bridge, or Hadfield, direct, and Manchester (Piccadilly) via Ardwick Junction
	Manchester (Oxford Road) and Ditton Junction
78	Hadfield or Glossop and Manchester (Piccadilly) via Ardwick Junction
	Warrington (Bank Quay) and Ditton Junction
79	Stalybridge and Manchester (Piccadilly) via Guide Bridge and Ardwick Junction
	Crewe and Warrington (Bank Quay)
84	Manchester (Piccadilly) and Manchester (Oxford Road)
94	Manchester (Exchange) and Stalybridge, Mossley or Greenfield
95	Manchester (Victoria) and Stalybridge, Mossley or Greenfield
96	Manchester (Exchange) and Huddersfield
97	Manchester (Victoria) and Leeds (City) via Huddersfield
98	Manchester (Exchange) and Leeds (City) via Huddersfield

Eastern Region

The Eastern Region uses the standard four-character headcode on many of its electric and diesel locomotives and multiple-units, throughout the Great Eastern Line and increasingly on the Great Northern Line. Where the four-character panel indicator has not yet been fitted, the two-character panel carries simply the appropriate train or route number headed by a white bar. Where the four-character code includes the route number in the last two positions, the second character is either "O" for fast and medium-fast trains or "L" for stopping trains. Trains routed on lines for which no code has yet been allocated, carry "OO" in the third and fourth positions.

THIRD AND FOURTH CHARACTERS
GREAT EASTERN SUBURBAN LINES

Route No.	Destination
01	Fenchurch Street
02	Stratford (main)
03	Ilford
04	Chadwell Heath
05	Gidea Park
06	Brentwood
07	Shenfield
08	Southend and the Southminster branch
09	Chelmsford
10	Enfield Town
11	Cheshunt via Edmonton
12	Broxbourne via Edmonton
13	Hertford East via Edmonton

Route No.	Destination
14	Bishops Stortford via Edmonton
16	Seven Sisters and the Palace Gates branch
17	Wood Street
18	Chingford
19	Stratford (low level) and Fork sidings
20	Tottenham
21	Cheshunt via Tottenham
22	Broxbourne via Tottenham
23	Hertford East via Tottenham
24	Bishops Stortford via Tottenham
25	St. Margarets and the Buntingford branch
26	Northumberland Park
27	Woolwich North
29	Elsenham
30	Marks Tey
31	Colchester (direct)
32	Manningtree
33	The Parkeston and Harwich branch
34	St. Botolphs and Colchester (via St. Botolphs)
35	Wivenhoe and Brightlingsea
36	Thorpe-le-Soken
37	Clacton
38	Walton
39	Witham and the Maldon or Braintree branches
45	E.C.S. to Thornton Field
46	E.C.S. to Stratford Old Yard
47	E.C.S. to Channelsea
48	E.C.S. or light engines to Stratford diesel depot
49	E.C.S. to Ilford car sheds

GREAT NORTHERN SURBURBAN LINES

Route No.	Route
50	Broad Street, Moorgate or Kings Cross and Western sidings
51	Broad Street, Moorgate or Kings Cross and Finsbury Park carriage sidings
52	Broad Street, Moorgate or Kings Cross and Bounds Green
53	Moorgate and Kings Cross
54	Finsbury Park carriage sidings and Highbury Vale
55	Hertford (North) or Cuffley and Gordon Hill
56	Hertford (North) and Cuffley
57	Hatfield and St. Albans
58	Welwyn Garden City and Hertford (North)
59	E.C.S. beyond Hitchin (until June 1961)
60	Kings Cross and New Barnet
61	Kings Cross and Potters Bar
62	Kings Cross and Hatfield and the Dunstable branch
63	Kings Cross and Welwyn Garden City
64	Kings Cross and Hitchin
65	Kings Cross or Hitchin and Baldock or Royston
66	Kings Cross or Hitchin and Cambridge
67	Kings Cross and Gordon Hill
68	Kings Cross and Crews Hill to Hertford (North)
69	Kings Cross and Finsbury Park
70	Moorgate and New Barnet
71	Moorgate and Potters Bar
72	Moorgate and Hatfield and the Dunstable branch
73	Moorgate and Welwyn Garden City

Route No.	Route
74	Moorgate and Hitchin
75	Moorgate and Baldock or Royston
76	Moorgate and Cambridge
77	Moorgate and Gordon Hill
78	Moorgate and Crews Hill to Hertford (North)
79	Moorgate and Finsbury Park
80	Finsbury Park or Ferme Park and New Barnet
81	Finsbury Park or Ferme Park and Potters Bar
82	Finsbury Park or Ferme Park and Hatfield and the Dunstable branch
83	Finsbury Park or Ferme Park and Welwyn Garden City
84	Finsbury Park or Ferme Park and Hitchin
85	Finsbury Park or Ferme Park and Baldock or Royston
86	Finsbury Park or Ferme Park and Cambridge
87	Finsbury Park or Ferme Park and Gordon Hill
88	Finsbury Park or Ferme Park and Crews Hill to Hertford (North)
89	Hertford (North) and Hitchin
90	Broad Street and New Barnet
91	Broad Street and Potters Bar
92	Broad Street and Hatfield and the Dunstable branch
93	Broad Street and Welwyn Garden City
94	Broad Street and Hitchin
95	Broad Street and Baldock or Royston
96	Broad Street and Cambridge
97	Broad Street and Gordon Hill
98	Broad Street and Crews Hill to Hertford (North)
99	Hatfield and Dunstable

GREAT EASTERN EAST ANGLIAN LINES

Route No.	Route
10	Norwich and the Cromer line
11	Norwich and Yarmouth (Vauxhall) via Acle
12	Norwich and Yarmouth (Vauxhall) via Reedham
13	Norwich and Lowestoft
14	Norwich and King's Lynn or Hunstanton
15	Norwich and Dereham
16	Norwich and Wells-next-the-sea
17	Norwich and Thetford
19	Norwich and Ely
20	Cambridge and the Cromer line
21	Cambridge and Norwich
22	Cambridge and Yarmouth (Vauxhall)
23	Cambridge and Lowestoft
24	Cambridge and King's Lynn or Hunstanton
25	Cambridge and Bury St. Edmunds
26	Cambridge and March or Whitemoor
27	Cambridge and Peterborough
28	Cambridge and Ipswich
29	Cambridge and Ely
30	Peterborough and the Cromer line
31	Peterborough and Norwich
32	Peterborough and Yarmouth (Vauxhall)
33	Peterborough and Lowestoft
34	Peterborough and King's Lynn or Hunstanton
35	Peterborough and Bury St. Edmunds
36	Peterborough and March or Whitemoor
39	Peterborough and Ely
40	March or Whitemoor and the Cromer line
41	March or Whitemoor and Norwich

Route No.	Route
42	March or Whitemoor and Yarmouth (Vauxhall)
43	March or Whitemoor and Lowestoft
44	March or Whitemoor and King's Lynn or Hunstanton
45	March or Whitemoor and Bury St. Edmunds
49	March or Whitemoor and Ely
50	London, Chelmsford or intermediate stations and the Cromer line
51	London, Chelmsford or intermediate stations and Norwich
52	London, Chelmsford or intermediate stations and Yarmouth (South Town)
53	London, Chelmsford or intermediate stations and Lowestoft
54	London, Chelmsford or intermediate stations and Felixstowe
55	London, Chelmsford or intermediate stations and Bury St. Edmunds
56	London, Chelmsford or intermediate stations and March or Whitemoor
57	London, Chelmsford or intermediate stations and Peterborough
58	London, Chelmsford or intermediate stations and Ipswich
60	Witham or Colchester and the Cromer line
61	Witham or Colchester and Norwich
62	Witham or Colchester and Yarmouth (South Town)
63	Witham or Colchester and Lowestoft
64	Witham or Colchester and Felixstowe
65	Witham or Colchester and Bury St. Edmunds
66	Witham or Colchester and March or Whitemoor
67	Witham or Colchester and Peterborough
68	Witham or Colchester and Ipswich
69	Witham or Colchester and Cambridge
70	Ipswich and the Cromer line
71	Ipswich and Norwich
72	Ipswich and Yarmouth (South Town)
73	Ipswich and Lowestoft
74	Ipswich and Felixstowe
75	Ipswich and Bury St. Edmunds
76	Ipswich and March or Whitemoor
77	Ipswich and Peterborough
78	Ipswich and Harwich
79	Ipswich and Ely
80	London, Sawbridgeworth or intermediate stations and the Cromer line
81	London, Sawbridgeworth or intermediate stations and Norwich
82	London, Sawbridgeworth or intermediate stations and Yarmouth (Vauxhall)
83	London, Sawbridgeworth or intermediate stations and Lowestoft
84	London, Sawbridgeworth or intermediate stations and King's Lynn or Hunstanton
85	London, Sawbridgeworth or intermediate stations and Bury St. Edmunds
86	London, Sawbridgeworth or intermediate stations and March or Whitemoor
87	London, Sawbridgeworth or intermediate stations and Peterborough
88	London, Sawbridgeworth or intermediate stations and Audley End or Cambridge
89	London, Sawbridgeworth or intermediate stations and Ely
90	Bishops Stortford and the Cromer line
91	Bishops Stortford and Norwich
92	Bishops Stortford and Yarmouth (Vauxhall)
93	Bishops Stortford and Lowestoft
94	Bishops Stortford and King's Lynn or Hunstanton
95	Bishops Stortford and Bury St. Edmunds
96	Bishops Stortford and March or Whitemoor
97	Bishops Stortford and Peterborough
98	Bishops Stortford and Audley End or Cambridge
99	Bishops Stortford and Ely

Western Region

Since shortly after nationalisation the Western Region has displayed the train number of every regular running express train, particularly on Saturdays, in a metal frame on the smokebox door. Within the last few years this three-figure train number has been replaced by the two-figure train number which forms the second half of the standard four-character headcode, and the existing three-character frames have been used to carry the last three characters of the standard code. The first character, indicating the train's class, is not incorporated; instead, the British Railways standard headlamp code is carried to supplement the three-character panel indication. All new Western Region diesel locomotives, however, are fitted with four-character frames.

REGIONAL AREA CODE

Code	Destination Area
A	London Area
B	Bristol District
C	Exeter and Plymouth Districts
F	Cardiff and Swansea Districts
H	Birmingham and Worcester Districts
J	Chester and Oswestry Districts
T	Newport and Gloucester Districts

Every Western Region train today carries a train or route identification number, no matter what its class or its importance. Individual train numbers are too numerous to list, but we give below the route numbers used on the Western Region where traffic is dense, notably in the Birmingham and London suburban areas. Note that Western Region route numbers, unlike route numbers on other Regions, refer only to the destination area (i.e. the train terminates between the two stated stations) and give no indication of the original starting point. The Western Region is divided into ten areas, shown below. Class 1 trains are numbered from 00 and Class 2 from 50.

LONDON AREA

Class 1 trains	Class 2 trains	Route
00	50	Paddington (Main) to Hayes
01	51	Paddington (Suburban) to Hayes
02	52	Paddington (Main) to West Drayton
03	53	Paddington (Suburban) to West Drayton
04	54	Paddington (Main) to Staines West
05	55	Paddington (Suburban) to Staines West
06	56	Paddington (Main) to Slough

Class 1 trains	Class 2 trains	Route
07	57	Paddington (Suburban) to Slough
08	58	Paddington (Main) to Windsor
09	59	Paddington (Surburban) to Windsor
10	60	Paddington (Main) to Maidenhead, Bourne End, High Wycombe and Aylesbury
11	61	Paddington (Suburban) to Maidenhead, Bourne End, High Wycombe and Aylesbury
12	62	Paddington (Main) to Henley-on-Thames
13	63	Paddington (Suburban) to Henley-on-Thames
14	64	Paddington (Main) to Reading General
15	65	Paddington (Suburban) to Reading General
16	66	Paddington to West Ruislip
17	67	West Ruislip to High Wycombe
18	68	High Wycombe to Princes Risborough
19	69	Princes Risborough to Bicester (North)
20	70	Paddington (Main) to Ealing Broadway
21	71	Paddington (Suburban) to Ealing Broadway
22	72	Ealing Broadway to Southall
23	73	Southall to Slough
24	74	Slough to Reading General
25	75	Reading General to Didcot
26	76	Didcot to Swindon
27	77	Didcot to Oxford
28	78	Oxford to Princes Risborough
29	79	Oxford to Bicester (London Road)
30	80	Ealing Broadway to Greenford
31	81	West Drayton to Uxbridge (Vine Street)
32	82	West Drayton to Staines (West)
33	83	Slough to Windsor and Eton
34	84	Maidenhead to High Wycombe
35	85	Bourne End to Marlow
36	86	Twyford to Henley-on-Thames
37	87	Reading to Newbury
38	88	Newbury to Westbury
40	90	Oxford to Kingham
41	91	Didcot to Newbury
42	92	Radley to Abingdon
43	93	Oxford to Fairford
44	94	Princes Risborough to Aylesbury
48	98	Bicester (North) to Banbury
49	99	Oxford to Banbury
—	96	E.C.S. to Old Oak Common
—	97	E.C.S. to West London C.S.

To and from the Southern Region, to be prefixed 2A:—

—	02	Reading to Basingstoke
—	03	Reading to Bournemouth West
—	04	Reading to Weymouth
—	18	Reading to Eastleigh and Southampton
—	52	Reading to Portsmouth Harbour
—	63	Reading to Portsmouth and Southsea
—	78	Reading to Southampton or Fawley
—	79	Reading to Lymington Pier

To and from the Midland Region:—

—	50	Marylebone to West Ruislip
—	51	Marylebone to High Wycombe
—	52	Marylebone to Princes Risborough
—	53	Marylebone to Woodford via Ashendon
—	54	Marylebone to Woodford via Aylesbury
—	79	Oxford to the L.M.R.

BRISTOL DISTRICT

Class 1 trains	Class 2 trains	Section of Route
01	51	Bristol (Temple Meads) to Avonmouth Dock via Clifton Down
02	52	Bristol (Temple Meads) to St. Andrews Road via Clifton Down
03	53	Bristol (Temple Meads) to Henbury via Clifton Down
04	54	Bristol (Temple Meads) to Severn Beach via Clifton Down
05	55	Bristol (Temple Meads) to Pilning (L.L.) via Clifton Down
06	56	Bristol (Temple Meads) to Henbury via Filton Junction
07	57	Bristol (Temple Meads) to St. Andrews Road via Henbury
08	58	Bristol (Temple Meads) to Avonmouth Dock via Henbury
09	59	Bristol (Temple Meads) to Pilning (H.L.) via Filton Junction
10	60	Bristol (Temple Meads) to Pilning (L.L.) via Filton Junction
11	61	Bristol (Temple Meads) to Severn Beach via Pilning (L.L.)
12	62	Bristol (Temple Meads) to St. Andrews Road via Pilning (L.L.)
13	63	Bristol (Temple Meads) to Avonmouth Dock via Pilning (L.L.)
—	64	E.C.S. to Malago Vale C.S.
—	65	E.C.S. to Marsh Junction and St. Philips Marsh
—	66	E.C.S. to Marsh Ponds C.S.
—	67	E.C.S. to Dr. Days Bridge sidings
—	68	E.C.S. from the L.M.R. to Lawrence Hill C.S.
19	69	Pilning (H.L.) to Severn Tunnel Junction
20	70	Bristol (Temple Meads) to Bath Spa
21	71	Bath Spa to Chippenham
22	72	Bath Spa to Trowbridge
23	73	Trowbridge to Westbury
24	74	Bristol (Temple Meads) to Gloucester
25	75	Chippenham to Swindon
26	76	Swindon to Didcot
27	77	Lawrence Hill to Swindon
28	78	Bristol to Lawrence Hill
29	79	Swindon to Kemble
30	80	Swindon (Town) to Cheltenham (St. James)
31	81	Swindon to Andover Junction
32	82	Swindon to Highworth
32	82	Kemble to Gloucester (Central)
33	83	Chippenham to Calne
33	83	Kemble to Cirencester (Town)
34	84	Kemble to Tetbury
35	85	Yatton to Witham and Frome
36	86	Yatton to Clevedon
37	87	Evercreech Junction to Highbridge
38	88	Westbury to Newbury
39	89	Patney and Chirton to Holt Junction
40	90	Castle Cary to Weymouth
41	91	Westbury to Salisbury
42	92	Bath (Green Park) to Templecombe
43	93	Bristol (Temple Meads) to Bath Green Park
44	94	Trowbridge to Chippenham
45	95	Bristol (Temple Meads) to Portishead
46	96	Bristol (Temple Meads) to Weston-Super-Mare

Class 1 trains	Class 2 trains	Section of Route
47	97	Weston-Super-Mare to Taunton
48	98	Westbury to Taunton (direct)
49	99	Westbury to Taunton (via Durston)

To and from the London Midland Region:—

—	70	Bristol to L.M.R. via Redditch and Barnt Green
—	72	Bristol to L.M.R. via Dunhampstead and Barnt Green
—	74	L.M.R. to Bristol via Barnt Green
—	75	Bristol to L.M.R. via Worcester (S.H.) and Barnt Green

E.C.S. movements between the following points:—

—	70	Marsh Junction, St. Philips Marsh and Marsh Pond to Bristol via North Somerset Junction
—	78	Dr. Days Bridge sidings to Bristol
—	93	Lawrence Hill Junction to Bristol
—	96	Malago Vale to Bristol
—	96	Marsh Junction, St. Philips Marsh and Marsh Pond to Bristol via Bristol West

EXETER DISTRICT

Class 1 trains	Class 2 trains	Section of Route
25	75	Newton Abbot to Plymouth
26	76	Newton Abbot to Exeter
27	77	Exeter to Taunton
30	80	Taunton to Yeovil (direct)
31	81	Taunton to Yeovil (via Durston)
32	82	Taunton to Chard Junction
33	83	Taunton to Minehead
34	84	Taunton to Barnstaple
35	85	Tiverton Junction to Hemyock
36	86	Tiverton Junction to Tiverton
37	87	Exeter to Dulverton
38	88	Exeter (St. Davids) to Exmouth Junction
40	90	Newton Abbot to Paignton
41	91	Paignton to Kingswear
42	92	Churston to Brixham
47	97	Taunton to Weston-Super-Mare
48	98	Taunton to Westbury (direct)
49	99	Taunton to Westbury (via Durston)

Southern Region trains running over Western Region lines carry the code C50 down and C51 up, prefixed by the normal Western classification number

PLYMOUTH DISTRICT

Class 1 trains	Class 2 trains	Section of Route
02	52	Chacewater to Newquay
03	53	Truro to Falmouth
04	54	Par to Newquay
05	55	Lostwithiel to Fowey
06	56	Bodmin Road to Bodmin General
07	57	Liskeard to Looe
08	58	Plymouth to Launceston
09	59	Brent to Kingsbridge
10	60	St. Erth to St. Ives
11	61	Gwinear Road to Helston
12	62	Bodmin General to Southern Region
13	63	Millbay Docks to Plymouth

Class 1 trains	Class 2 trains	Section of Route
—	65	E.C.S. to and from Laira Junction
—	66	E.C.S. to and from Plymouth (Friary)
—	67	E.C.S. to and from Plymouth (Millbay)
20	70	Penzance to Chacewater
21	71	Chacewater to Truro
22	72	Truro to Doublebois
23	73	Doublebois to Saltash
24	74	Saltash to Plymouth
25	75	Plymouth to Newton Abbot

For Southern Region trains running over Western Region lines the code C50 is used for all down trains and C51 is used for all up trains, prefixed by the normal Western Region classification number

NEWPORT DISTRICT

Class 1 trains	Class 2 trains	Section of Route
02	52	Newport to Cardiff
11	61	Hereford to Shrewsbury
12	62	Newport to Brynmawr
13	63	Aberbeeg to Ebbw Vale
14	64	Ebbw Vale to Beaufort
19	69	Severn Tunnel Junction to Pilning
32	82	Hereford to Ledbury
35	85	Brecon to Hereford
		Newport to Chepstow
36	86	Chepstow to Gloucester
37	87	Newport to Llantarnam Junction
38	88	Llantarnam Junction to Panteg
39	89	Panteg to Blaenavon
40	90	Hereford to Gloucester
		Llantarnam Junction to Pontypool Road
41	91	Abergavenny to Hereford
42	92	Pontypool Road to Abergavenny
43	93	Pontypool Road to Glascoed R.O.F.
44	94	Panteg to Pontypool Road
45	95	Hengoed to Pontypool Road
46	96	Newport to Bargoed
—	97	E.C.S. to Newport (Ebbw Junction) C.S.

SWANSEA DISTRICT

Class 1 trains	Class 2 trains	Section of Route
00	50	Margam to Pyle
01	51	Margam to Porthcawl
05	55	Duffryn Rhondda to Treherbert
13	63	Swansea to Pontardulais
14	64	Llanelly to Pantyffynnon
15	65	Pantyffynnon to Llandilo
17	67	Llandilo to Llandovery
18	68	Llandovery to Shrewsbury
19	69	Port Talbot to Duffryn Rhondda
20	70	Briton Ferry to Duffryn Rhondda
21	71	Cymmer Corrwg to North Rhondda
22	72	Swansea (High Street) to Felin Fran
23	73	Whitland to Cardigan
24	74	Whitland to Pembroke Dock

Class 1 trains	Class 2 trains	Section of Route
26	76	Clarbeston Road to Fishguard Harbour
27	77	Carmarthen to Aberystwyth
29	79	Colbren Junction to Brecon
30	80	Neath (Riverside) to Colbren Junction
35	85	Neath Junction to Neath (Riverside)
36	86	Glyn Neath to Rhigos Halt
37	87	Resolven to Glyn Neath
38	88	Neath General to Resolven
39	89	Margam to Port Talbot
40	90	Port Talbot to Briton Ferry
41	91	Briton Ferry to Neath (General)
42	92	Neath (General) to Swansea (High Street)
43	93	Swansea (High Street) to Llanelly
44	94	Llanelly to Carmarthen
45	95	Carmarthen to Whitland
46	96	Whitland to Neyland
47	97	Johnston to Milford Haven

CARDIFF DISTRICT

Class 1 trains	Class 2 trains	Section of Route
00	50	Margam to Pyle
01	51	Margam to Porthcawl
02	52	Newport to Cardiff (General)
03	53	Cardiff (General) to Bridgend
04	54	Bridgend to Pyle
05	55	Duffryn Rhondda to Treherbert
06	56	Cardiff (General) to Penarth
07	57	Penarth to Barry
08	58	Cardiff (General) to Barry via Dinas
09	59	Barry to Llantwit Major
10	60	Llantwit Major to Bridgend
		Merthyr to Pontsticill Junction
11	61	Barry to Barry Island
12	62	Cardiff (Bute Road) to Cardiff (Queen Street)
13	63	Cardiff (Queen Street) to Caerphilly
14	64	Cardiff (Bute Road) to Coryton
15	65	Caerphilly to Caerphilly Works
16	66	Caerphilly to Ystrad Mynach
17	67	Caerphilly to Senghenydd
18	68	Ystrad Mynach to Nelson
		Abergoed to New Tredegar
19	69	Nelson to Dowlais (Cae Harris)
20	70	Ystrad Mynach to Bargoed
21	71	Bargoed to Rhymney
22	72	Bargoed to Brecon
23	73	Aberdare (H.L.) to Hengoed (H.L.)
24	74	Cardiff (General) to Cardiff (Clarence Road)
25	75	Cardiff (General) to Cardiff (Queen Street)
26	76	Cardiff (Queen Street) to Pontypridd
27	77	Pontypridd to Abercynon
28	78	Abercynon to Merthyr
29	79	Abercynon to Aberdare
30	80	Pontypridd to Treherbert
31	81	Porth to Maerdy
		Brecon to Builth Road
32	82	Barry to Pontypridd via Wenvoe
33	83	Tondu to Porthcawl

Class 1 trains	Class 2 trains	Section of Route
33	83	Rhigos Halt to Aberdare (H.L.)
34	84	Tremains Platform to Blaengwynfi
		Hirwaun to Merthyr
35	85	Brecon to Hereford
—	98	E.C.S. to Cardiff (Cathays) C.S.
—	99	E.C.S. to Cardiff (Canton) C.S.

GLOUCESTER DISTRICT

Class 1 trains	Class 2 trains	Section of Route
21	71	Ashchurch to Redditch
23	73	Gloucester (Eastgate) to Worcester (Shrub Hill)
24	74	Gloucester (Eastgate) to Bristol (Temple Meads)
28	78	Hartlebury to Worcester (Foregate Street)
29	79	Worcester (Foregate Street) to Henwick
30	80	Cheltenham (St. James) to Swindon Town
		Henwick to Great Malvern
31	81	Cheltenham (St. James) to Gloucester (Central)
		Great Malvern to Ledbury
32	82	Gloucester (Central) to Kemble
		Ledbury to Hereford
34	84	Stratford-on-Avon to Honeybourne
35	85	Honeybourne to Cheltenham (St. James)
36	86	Kingham to Moreton-in-Marsh
		Chepstow to Gloucester (Central)
37	87	Moreton-in-Marsh to Honeybourne
		Ashchurch to Upton-on-Severn
38	88	Honeybourne to Evesham
39	89	Evesham to Worcester (Shrub Hill)
40	90	Kingham to Oxford
		Gloucester (Central) to Hereford
41	91	Worcester (Shrub Hill) to Bromyard
		Kingham to Chipping Norton
42	92	Kingham to Cheltenham (St. James)
45	95	Coaley Junction to Dursley
46	96	Berkeley Road to Lydney (Town)

TO AND FROM THE LONDON MIDLAND REGION

Class 1 trains	Class 2 trains	Section of Route
—	70	W.R. to L.M.R. via Redditch and Barnt Green
—	71	L.M.R. to Ashchurch via Redditch
—	72	W.R. to L.M.R. via Dunhampstead and Barnt Green
—	73	L.M.R. to Gloucester (Eastgate) via Barnt Green and Stoke Works Junction
—	75	L.M.R. to W.R. via Barnt Green, Stoke Works Junction and Worcester (Shrub Hill)
		L.M.R. to Worcester (Foregate Street) via Barnt Green and Stoke Works Junction
—	80	L.M.R. to Malvern Wells via Barnt Green and Stoke Works Junction

BIRMINGHAM DISTRICT

Class 1 trains	Class 2 trains	Section of Route
00	50	Shrewsbury to Wellington
01	51	Wellington to Wolverhampton (L.L.)
02	52	Wolverhampton to Birmingham (Snow Hill)

Class 1 trains	Class 2 trains	Section of Route
03	53	Birmingham (Snow Hill) to Solihull
04	54	Birmingham (Moor Street) to Solihull
05	55	Solihull to Lapworth
06	56	Lapworth to Leamington Spa
07	57	Leamington Spa to Banbury (General)
08	58	Birmingham (Moor Street) to Henley-in-Arden
09	59	Birmingham (Snow Hill) to Henley-in-Arden
10	60	Henley-in-Arden to Stratford-on-Avon
11	61	Stratford-on-Avon to Leamington Spa
12	62	Birmingham (Snow Hill) to Stourbridge Junction
13	63	Old Hill to Dudley
14	64	Birmingham (Snow Hill) to Dudley
		Dudley to Dudley Port (L.M.R.)
		Wellington to Stafford (L.M.R.)
15	65	Wolverhampton (L.L.) to Stourbridge Junction
		Wellington to Crewe (L.M.R.)
16	66	Stourbridge Junction to Stourbridge Town
		Shrewsbury to Stafford (L.M.R.)
—	67	E.C.S. to Queenshead C.S.
—	68	E.C.S. to Cannock Road C.S.
—	69	E.C.S. to Tyseley C.S.
24	74	Wellington to Much Wenlock
26	76	Hartlebury to Kidderminster
		Banbury Junction to Woodford Halse (L.M.R.)
27	77	Kidderminster to Stourbridge Junction
28	78	Hartlebury to Worcester (Foregate Street)
33	83	Bewdley to Woofferton
34	84	Stratford-on-Avon to Honeybourne
43	93	Kidderminster to Bewdley
44	94	Hartlebury to Bewdley
45	95	Bewdley to Arley
46	96	Arley to Bridgnorth
47	97	Bridgnorth to Shrewsbury
48	98	Banbury (General) to Bicester (North)
49	99	Banbury (General) to Oxford

SHREWSBURY DISTRICT

Class 1 trains	Class 2 trains	Section of Route
00	50	Wellington to Shrewsbury
02	52	Shrewsbury to Wrexham (General)
03	53	Barmouth to Wrexham (General)
04	54	Wrexham to Chester
05	55	Chester to Birkenhead
07	57	Shrewsbury to Welshpool
08	58	Gobowen to Oswestry
09	59	Bala Junction to Bala
11	61	Shrewsbury to Hereford
18	68	Shrewsbury to Llandovery
21	71	Wrexham (Central) to Ellesmere
22	72	Whitchurch to Oswestry
23	73	Oswestry to Welshpool
24	74	Welshpool to Moat Lane Junction
25	75	Moat Lane Junction to Machynlleth
26	76	Machynlleth to Aberystwyth
27	77	Aberystwyth to Carmarthen
31	81	Builth Wells to Brecon
36	86	Dovey Junction to Barmouth

Class 1 trains	Class 2 trains	Section of Route
37	87	Barmouth to Portmadoc
38	88	Portmadoc to Afon Wen
39	89	Afon Wen to Pwllheli
43	93	Moat Lane Junction to Builth Wells
47	97	Shrewsbury to Bridgnorth
49	99	Llanymynech to Llanfyllin

TO AND FROM THE LONDON MIDLAND REGION

Class 2 trains	Section of Route
50	Birkenhead and Chester to Wellington
52	Birkenhead and Chester to Shrewsbury via Ruabon
53	Birkenhead and Chester to Barmouth
54	Western Region to Chester
55	Western Region to Birkenhead
66	Shrewsbury to Stafford (in both directions)
67	Shrewsbury to Crewe (in both directions)
78	Wrexham to Harwarden Bridge (in both directions)
79	New Brighton to Wrexham (in both directions)
80	Wrexham to Chester (in both directions)
81	Pwllheli to Bangor
83	Afon Wen to Bangor
84	Penychain to Llandudno
89	Birkenhead or Chester to Pwllheli via Ruabon

Light Engines

The Western Region prefixes code numbers with the letter Z to denote light engines returning or being transferred to a locomotive running-shed or maintenance depot. Space permits us to list only the main codes in use on the Region and not all the local codes in individual areas.

Regional Light Engine Code Numbers

Code	Destination	Code	Destination
Z20	Old Oak Common	Z39	Penzance
Z21	Slough	Z40	Plymouth (Friary)
Z22	Southall	Z41	Wolverhampton (Stafford Road)
Z23	Reading	Z42	Oxley
Z24	Didcot	Z43	Banbury
Z25	Oxford	Z44	Leamington Spa
Z26	Bristol (Bath Road)	Z45	Tyseley
Z27	Bristol (St. Philips Marsh)	Z46	Stourbridge Junction
Z28	Swindon	Z47	Shrewsbury
Z29	Westbury	Z48	Wellington (Salop)
Z30	Bristol (Barrow Road)	Z49	Croes Newydd
Z31	Bath (S. and D.)	Z51	Worcester
Z32	Templecombe	Z52	Gloucester
Z33	Newton Abbot	Z53	Hereford
Z34	Taunton	Z54	Kidderminster
Z35	Exeter	Z55	Gloucester
Z36	Laira	Z56	Bromsgrove
Z37	St. Blazey	Z57	Newport (Ebbw Vale)
Z38	Truro	Z58	Newport (Pill)

Code	Destination	Code	Destination
Z59	Cardiff (Canton)	Z73	Carmarthen
Z60	Llantrisant	Z74	Neyland
Z61	Severn Tunnel Junction	Z75	Fishguard
Z62	Tondu	Z77	Cardiff (Cathays)
Z63	Pontypool Road	Z78	Radyr Junction
Z64	Aberbeeg	Z79	Cardiff (East Dock)
Z65	Aberdare	Z80	Barry
Z67	Neath	Z81	Merthyr
Z68	Duffryn Yard	Z82	Abercynon
Z69	Danygraig	Z83	Treherbert
Z70	Swansea	Z84	Oswestry
Z71	Landore	Z86	Machynlleth
Z72	Llanelly		

When light engines are being transferred from one district to another, the following codes are used:—

Z88	London District	Z93	Newport District
Z89	Bristol District	Z94	Cardiff District
Z90	Exeter District	Z95	Swansea District
Z91	Plymouth District	Z96	Birmingham District
Z92	Gloucester District	Z97	Shrewsbury District

SPECIAL HEADCODES

Universal headcodes have also been instituted for special departmental trains:

Code	Description
1Z01	Inspection train, not stopping in section
2Z01	Diesel cars and lightweight railbuses which cannot be relied upon to work track circuits
6Z01	Weed-killing train
8Z02	Out of gauge load train which can pass another out of gauge load train similarly signalled on adjoining line
8Z03	Out of gauge load train which cannot pass another out of gauge load train similarly signalled on adjoining line
8Z04	Out of gauge load train which requires the adjoining line to be blocked
1Z99	Breakdown or snow-plough train going to clear the line
2Z99	Breakdown or snow-plough train not going to clear the line
1X01 } 1X02 } 1X03 }	Royal Train, according to priority

TWO-CHARACTER CODES

By far the most extensively used of British Railways panel codes embody only two characters, whose significance varies in individual Regions. The Southern Region has a code number for every electric or diesel route on each of its three sections, and the Scottish Region uses a similar double-number code on its electric trains. The usual practice on the other Regions is to indicate the route by the second character only, the first being used to indicate the class of train (see page 21).

A two-character code used in a four-character area displays a white bar across the top of the route number.

Southern Electric and Diesel Headcodes

Since the first multiple-unit electric scheme was introduced on the London, Brighton and South Coast Railway in 1909, the "Southern Electric" sets have utilised code letters or numbers to distinguish the many different routes over which they run. At first, letter codes were most widely used, but the L.B.S.C.R.'s South London line always used a number code. The code letter was often the initial of the destination station; thus H stood for Hampton Court and S for Shepperton. However, as more and more lines were electrified it became increasingly difficult to find a different code designation for every route. The Southern Railway therefore decided to amplify the basic code by the introduction of a "dot", "double dot" and "dash" stencil frame, fixed above the ordinary letter code.

The 4-LAV units used on the newly electrified Brighton line in 1933 were the first to carry a new, comprehensive number code. All new main line units appearing after this date carried code numbers, although the original units retained letters; and the system was extended to suburban services on the introduction of the first all-steel stock in 1942. The diesel locomotives and multiple-units introduced under the British Railways Modernisation scheme also used the number code. Over the years, most of the older stock has been withdrawn, until today only a handful of letter-carrying units survive.

Note that the same number series is used by each of the three sections of the Southern Region and also on the Hampshire diesel multiple-units.

Southern Electric and Diesel-Electric Headcodes

WESTERN SECTION

Numeral Codes		Route
2	Waterloo and Portsmouth Harbour (special)	Chertsey
2	Eastleigh and Fawley	
3	Waterloo and Portsmouth & Southsea	Bookham
4	Waterloo and Portsmouth Harbour	Bookham
5	Waterloo and Portsmouth & Southsea ...	Cobham
6	Waterloo and Portsmouth Harbour	Cobham
7	Waterloo and Portsmouth & Southsea (slow) (with Alton portion on rear, detached at Woking)	Worplesdon
7	Woking and Portsmouth & Southsea (slow) (detached from or attached to Waterloo train at Woking)	Worplesdon

7	Alton to Woking ... ... (Up trains coupling at Woking)	
8	Waterloo and Portsmouth Harbour ... ... (semi-fast, not stopping at Havant)	Worplesdon
9	Waterloo and Portsmouth & Southsea (Special)	Chertsey
10	Waterloo and Woking	Earlsfield
10	Southampton Terminus and Winchester (Chesil)	
12	Waterloo and Alton ... ... (with Portsmouth portion on rear detached at Woking)	Earlsfield
12	Woking to Alton ... ... (detached at Woking from Waterloo train)	
12	Southampton Terminus and Southampton Central	
12	Southampton and Romsey or Andover Junc.	Nursling
13	Waterloo and Woking	Chertsey
13	Salisbury and Southampton Terminus ...	Eastleigh
14	Waterloo and Virginia Water	Weybridge
14	Southampton Terminus and Andover Junc. ...	Eastleigh
15	Southampton Terminus and Salisbury ...	Nursling
15	Waterloo and Alton (special)	Chertsey
16	Waterloo and Effingham Junc. or Guildford	Epsom
16	Southampton Terminus and Alton	
17	Waterloo and Weybridge	Brentford
17	Staines and Windsor ... ... (detached from or attached to a train via Brentford)	
17	Waterloo and Horsham	Motspur Park
18	Waterloo and Chessington South	Motspur Park
18	Waterloo and Weybridge	Richmond
18	Staines and Windsor ... ... (detached from or attached to a train via Richmond)	
18	Southampton Terminus, Eastleigh and Winchester City	
19	Waterloo and Worcester Park, Epsom or Leatherhead	Motspur Park
20	Waterloo and Ascot	Earlsfield and Woking
20	Guildford and Farnham or Alton	
21	Guildford and Aldershot	
24	Waterloo and Shepperton	Wimbledon
25	Waterloo and Woking	Brentford and Ascot
26	Waterloo and Woking	Richmond and Ascot
27	Waterloo and Reading, Aldershot or Farnham	Brentford
28	Waterloo and Reading, Aldershot or Farnham	Richmond
30	Waterloo and Hampton Court	
32	Waterloo and Alton	Earlsfield
35	Portsmouth and Gillingham (special) ...	Guildford and Epsom
37	Waterloo and Alton	Brentford and Ascot

38	Waterloo and Alton	Richmond and Ascot
41	Reading and Bognor or Littlehampton (special)	Ascot, Aldershot Guildford, Havant
42	Portsmouth Harbour and Southampton Central (stopping)	Netley
42	Reading and Bognor or Littlehampton (special)	Chertsey, Worplesdon, Havant
42	Waterloo and Effingham Junc. or Guildford ...	Cobham
43	Portsmouth & Southsea and Southampton Central (stopping)	Netley
44	Portsmouth Harbour and Salisbury (stopping)	Netley
45	Portsmouth & Southsea and Salisbury (stopping)	Netley
46	Portsmouth Harbour and Andover Junc. (stopping)	Netley
47	Portsmouth & Southsea and Andover Junc. (stopping)	Netley
47	Waterloo and Shepperton	Richmond
48	Portsmouth Harbour and Southampton Terminus (stopping)	Netley
49	Portsmouth & Southsea and Southampton Terminus (stopping)	Netley
52	Waterloo and Aldershot or Farnham (stopping at Surbiton)	Earlsfield
52	Aldershot or Farnham to Waterloo	Earlsfield
52	Portsmouth Harbour and Winchester City ...	Eastleigh
53	Waterloo and Aldershot or Farnham	East Putney
54	Barnes and Bognor or Littlehampton (special)	Chertsey, Worplesdon, Havant
54	Portsmouth Harbour and Salisbury	Botley
56	Portsmouth Harbour and Andover Junc. or Salisbury	Botley and Fullerton
57	Waterloo and Portsmouth & Southsea (slow)	Worplesdon
57	Waterloo and Windsor	Brentford
58	Waterloo and Windsor	Richmond
58	Portsmouth Harbour and Alton	Eastleigh
61	Waterloo (M.L.) to Waterloo (W.L.) ...	Teddington
62	Waterloo (W.L.) to Waterloo (M.L.) ...	Teddington
62	Wimbledon to Waterloo	Earlsfield
63	Waterloo (M.L.) and Strawberry Hill ...	Kingston
63	Portsmouth & Southsea or Fareham and Winchester City	Botley
64	Waterloo (W.L.) and Strawberry Hill ...	Richmond
65	Waterloo, Wimbledon and Littlehampton (special)	Epsom
65	Portsmouth & Southsea and Salisbury ...	Botley and Dean
65	Portsmouth & Southsea and Eastleigh or Romsey	Botley
67	Wimbledon and Bognor (special)	Epsom

67	Portsmouth & Southsea and Andover Junc. or Salisbury	Botley and Fullerton
68	Waterloo and Kingston	Richmond
68	Windsor and Bognor or Littlehampton (special)	Chertsey, Worplesdon, Havant
69	Wimbledon and Bognor (special)	Epsom, Littlehampton
69	Portsmouth & Southsea and Alton	Eastleigh
70	Waterloo and Portsmouth & Southsea (semi-fast, stopping at Havant)	Worplesdon
71	Waterloo and Portsmouth & Southsea (semi-fast, not stopping at Havant)	Worplesdon
72	Waterloo and Aldershot or Farnham ... ... (not stopping at Surbiton)	Earlsfield
72	Southampton Central and Winchester (Chesil)	
74	Southampton Central and Andover Junc. ...	Eastleigh
76	Southampton Central and Alton	
78	Southampton Central—Eastleigh—Winchester City—Basingstoke	
80	Waterloo and Portsmouth Harbour ... ... (semi-fast, stopping at Havant)	Worplesdon
81	Waterloo and Portsmouth Harbour (slow) ...	Worplesdon
81	Woking and Portsmouth Harbour (slow) ... (detached from or attached to Waterloo train at Woking)	Worplesdon
82	Portsmouth Harbour and Southampton Central (semi-fast)	Netley
83	Portsmouth & Southsea and Southampton Central (semi-fast)	Netley
84	Portsmouth Harbour and Salisbury (semi-fast)	Netley
85	Portsmouth & Southsea and Salisbury (semi-fast)	Netley
86	Hampton Court or Shepperton and Waterloo (special)	East Putney
86	Waterloo and Wimbledon	East Putney
86	Portsmouth Harbour and Andover Junc. (semi-fast)	Netley
87	Waterloo (W.L.) to Waterloo (W.L.) ...	Richmond-Brentford
87	Portsmouth & Southsea and Andover Junc. (semi-fast)	Netley
88	Portsmouth Harbour and Southampton Terminus (semi-fast)	Netley
89	Portsmouth & Southsea and Southampton Terminus (semi-fast)	Netley
89	Waterloo (W.L.) to Waterloo (W.L.) ...	Brentford-Richmond
02	Waterloo and Alton	East Putney
03	Windsor and Portsmouth & Southsea (special)	Worplesdon
03	Basingstoke and Bournemouth West	Sway
04	Windsor and Portsmouth Harbour (special)	Worplesdon
05	Waterloo and Portsmouth & Southsea (special)	East Putney and Worplesdon

06	Waterloo and Portsmouth Harbour (special)	East Putney and Worplesdon
07	Waterloo and Portsmouth & Southsea (non-stop)	Worplesdon
08	Waterloo and Portsmouth Harbour (non-stop)	Worplesdon
09	Waterloo and Ascot (special)	Weybridge and Chertsey

Empty trains carry relevant numeral route indicator with a bar thereover except as follows:—

1̄3̄	Virginia Water or Chertsey and Woking ...	
1̄4̄	Farnham and Alton	
1̄4̄	Fratton and Portsmouth & Southsea	
1̄5̄	Durnsford Road to Effingham Junc.	Epsom
1̄5̄	Chertsey and Farnham	Woking
1̄5̄	Leatherhead and Bookham	
1̄7̄	Waterloo and Weybridge	Brentford
1̄7̄	Hounslow and Feltham	
1̄8̄	Waterloo or Durnsford Road to Chessington South	
1̄8̄	Twickenham and Feltham	
1̄8̄	Waterloo and Weybridge	Richmond
2̄3̄	Waterloo and Farnham	Hounslow and Camberley
2̄3̄	Effingham Junc. and Farnham	Guildford
2̄4̄	Durnsford Road to Shepperton	
2̄9̄	Waterloo and Farnham	Twickenham and Camberley
3̄0̄	Waterloo or Durnsford Road to Hampton Court	
3̄4̄	All stations except Brighton or Lovers Walk to Durnsford Road	
4̄2̄	Effingham Junc. and Guildford	
4̄7̄	Waterloo to Shepperton	Richmond
4̄7̄	Strawberry Hill to Shepperton	
6̄1̄	Teddington or Strawberry Hill to Waterloo (W.L.)	Richmond
6̄2̄	Durnsford Road to Teddington or Strawberry Hill	
6̄2̄	Waterloo to Strawberry Hill	Earlsfield or Richmond
6̄2̄	Waterloo to Teddington	Earlsfield
6̄2̄	Shepperton to Strawberry Hill	
6̄2̄	Strawberry Hill to Waterloo (M.L.)	Earlsfield
7̄2̄	Waterloo to Farnham	Earlsfield
8̄6̄	Hampton Court or Shepperton to Waterloo	East Putney
8̄7̄	Waterloo to Hounslow	Richmond
8̄7̄	Hounslow to Waterloo	Brentford
8̄9̄	Waterloo to Hounslow	Brentford
8̄9̄	Hounslow to Waterloo	Richmond

0̄1̄	Farnham and Fratton, Portsmouth & Southsea or Portsmouth Harbour	Aldershot and Guildford
0̄1̄	Waterloo to Durnsford Road	Wimbledon "C" Box or Worcester Park
0̄2̄	Fratton and Portsmouth Harbour	
0̄3̄	Waterloo to Wimbledon Park	East Putney
0̄3̄	Wimbledon Park to Waterloo	East Putney
0̄4̄	Brighton or Lovers Walk to Durnsford Road	
0̄4̄	Durnsford Road to Lancing	
0̄7̄	Waterloo to Fratton	

CENTRAL SECTION

N.B. The Quarry line is between Coulsdon and Earlswood, avoiding Redhill

1	Brighton and West Worthing	
1	Arundel and Littlehampton	
1	Eastbourne and Ore	
1	Lewes and Seaford	
1	Horsted Keynes and Haywards Heath ...	
1	Barnham and Bognor	
1	Preston Park and Brighton	
2	Redhill and Reigate	
2	Horsted Keynes and Brighton	
2	Three Bridges and Horsham	
2	Polegate and Eastbourne	
2	London Bridge and Victoria	South London line
2	West Croydon and Wimbledon	Mitcham Junc.
2	Purley and Tattenham Corner (shuttle service only)	
3	Purley and Caterham (shuttle service only)	
3	London Bridge and Brighton (fast)	Quarry
3	Arundel and Bognor	Littlehampton
4	Victoria and Brighton (fast)	Quarry
4	Arundel and Bognor	Direct
5	London Bridge and Brighton (stopping) ...	Quarry
5	Three Bridges and Littlehampton	Direct
6	Victoria and Brighton (stopping)	Quarry
6	Three Bridges and Bognor	Direct
7	London Bridge and Brighton (special) ...	Tulse Hill, Crystal Palace and Quarry
8	Victoria and Brighton (slow)	Quarry
9	Three Bridges and Bognor	Littlehampton
10	Holborn Viaduct and Littlehampton (special)	Herne Hill, Streatham Common, Selhurst, Quarry and Horsham
10	Bognor Regis and Portsmouth & Southsea ...	
12	Bognor and Portsmouth Harbour	
12	Victoria and Brighton (semi-fast)	Redhill

13	London Bridge and Brighton (semi-fast) ...	Redhill
13	Littlehampton, Barnham and Portsmouth & Southsea	
14	Victoria and Brighton (slow)	Redhill
15	Chichester and Portsmouth & Southsea ...	
15	London Bridge and Brighton (slow)	Redhill
16	Victoria and Littlehampton	Quarry and Worthing
16	Brighton to Ore	Eastbourne
17	London Bridge and Littlehampton	Quarry and Worthing
17	Brighton and Lewes	
17	St. Helier to Blackfriars	Tulse Hill and Herne Hill
18	Victoria and Littlehampton	Redhill and Worthing
18	Ore to Brighton	Eastbourne
19	London Bridge and Littlehampton	Redhill and Worthing
20	Victoria and Portsmouth Harbour	Mitcham Junc.
21	London Bridge and Blackfriars or Holborn Viaduct	West Croydon and St. Helier
23	London Bridge and Portsmouth	Quarry and Horsham
24	Victoria and Brighton (fast)	Redhill
25	London Bridge and Portsmouth Harbour ...	Redhill and Horsham
26	Victoria and Portsmouth Harbour	Quarry and Horsham
26	Brighton and Hastings or Ore	Direct
28	Victoria and Portsmouth Harbour	Redhill and Horsham
28	Brighton and Seaford	
30	Victoria and West Croydon, Wallington or Sutton	Streatham Common
30	Brighton and Portsmouth Harbour	Littlehampton
31	London Bridge, West Croydon, Epsom and Horsham	Norwood Junc.
31	Brighton and Bognor Regis	Littlehampton
32	Holborn Viaduct and Brighton (special) ...	Herne Hill, Streatham Common, Selhurst and Quarry
32	Victoria and Selhurst	Streatham Common
32	Brighton and Tonbridge	Lewes and Uckfield
34	Victoria and Reigate	Redhill
34	Preston Park and Hove	
35	Brighton and Littlehampton	
35	London Bridge and Portsmouth & Southsea or Portsmouth Harbour	West Croydon and Effingham Junc.
35	London Bridge and Selhurst	Tulse Hill
36	Brighton and Eastbourne	
36	Victoria and Beckenham Junc.	Streatham Hill and Crystal Palace
37	London Bridge and Reigate	Redhill
37	Horsted Keynes, Haywards Heath and Seaford	

38	Tooting and Littlehampton	Wimbledon and Mitcham
38	Victoria and Tattenham Corner	Streatham Common and Purley
39	London Bridge and Epsom Downs	Norwood Junc. and West Croydon
40	Victoria and Bognor Regis	Mitcham Junc.
41	Victoria and Coulsdon North	Crystal Palace and East Croydon
41	Streatham Hill and Brighton (special) ...	Quarry
42	Bognor Regis to Victoria	Littlehampton, Horsham and Redhill
43	London Bridge and Bognor Regis	Quarry and Horsham
45	London Bridge and Bognor Regis	Redhill and Horsham
46	Victoria and Bognor Regis	Quarry and Horsham
46	Horsted Keynes, Haywards Heath and Lewes	
47	London Bridge and Bognor Regis	West Croydon
48	Victoria and Bognor Regis	Redhill and Horsham
49	Horsted Keynes, Haywards Heath and Eastbourne	
49	Tooting and Bognor Regis (not via Littlehampton)	Wimbledon and Mitcham
49	London Bridge to London Bridge	Sydenham, Crystal Palace and Tulse Hill
50	Victoria and Littlehampton	Mitcham Junc. and Horsham
51	Streatham Hill and Brighton (special) ...	Redhill
52	Victoria and Ore	Quarry and Eastbourne
54	Victoria and Ore (not via Eastbourne)	Quarry and Direct
56	London Bridge and Brighton (special) ...	Streatham and Quarry
57	London Bridge and Littlehampton	West Croydon and Horsham
58	Victoria and Littlehampton	Redhill and Horsham
59	London Bridge and Littlehampton	Redhill and Horsham
60	Brighton and Portsmouth Harbour (semi-fast)	Direct
61	London Bridge and Ore	Redhill and Eastbourne
62	Victoria and Eastbourne	Quarry
62	Brighton and Portsmouth Harbour (slow) ...	Direct
63	London Bridge and Ore	Quarry and Eastbourne
64	Victoria and Eastbourne	Redhill
64	Brighton and Bognor Regis	Direct
65	London Bridge and Eastbourne	Quarry
67	London Bridge and Eastbourne	Redhill
68	Victoria and Seaford	Quarry
69	London Bridge and Seaford	Quarry

71	London Bridge and Bognor Regis (special) ...	Tulse Hill, Crystal Palace, Sutton and Horsham
72	Victoria and Ore	Redhill and Eastbourne
73	London Bridge and Littlehampton (special) ...	Tulse Hill, Crystal Palace, Sutton and Horsham
75	London Bridge and Portsmouth Harbour ...	Redhill, Horsham and Littlehampton
76	Victoria and Newhaven Harbour	Quarry
78	Victoria and Newhaven Harbour	Redhill
80	Victoria and Caterham	Streatham Common and Purley
81	London Bridge and Caterham	
82	Victoria and Crystal Palace	Streatham Common, Selhurst and Norwood Junc.
83	London Bridge and Selhurst	Forest Hill
84	Victoria and Epsom Downs	Streatham Common and West Croydon
85	London Bridge and Tattenham Corner ...	
86	Victoria and Horsham	Mitcham Junc.
87	Streatham Hill and Bognor Regis (special) ...	Quarry and Horsham
89	Horsham and Billingshurst	
89	London Bridge and Dorking North, Horsham, Billingshurst or Chichester	Mitcham Junc.
90	Victoria and Bognor Regis	Mitcham Junc. and Littlehampton
90	London Bridge to London Bridge	Tulse Hill, Thornton Heath and Norwood Junc.
91	London Bridge and Bognor Regis	Mitcham Junc. and Littlehampton
92	Victoria and Bognor Regis	West Croydon
93	Charing Cross or Cannon Street to Caterham	
93	Tattenham Corner or Caterham to Cannon Street	
94	London Bridge to London Bridge	Tulse Hill, Crystal Palace (L.L.) and Sydenham
94	Victoria and Coulsdon North	Streatham Common and East Croydon
95	London Bridge and Bognor Regis	Redhill, Horsham and Littlehampton
96	Victoria and Bognor Regis	Quarry, Horsham and Littlehampton
97	Charing Cross and Reigate	Redhill
97	Brighton, Crawley and Horsham	Three Bridges
98	Victoria to Bognor Regis	Redhill, Horsham and Littlehampton
0	Victoria and Epsom Downs	Mitcham Junc.

01	Victoria and London Bridge	Streatham Hill and Tulse Hill
01	Charing Cross or Cannon Street to Tattenham Corner	
01	Tattenham Corner or Caterham to Charing Cross	
02	Victoria and Epsom or Guildford	Mitcham Junc.
03	London Bridge, Effingham Junc. and Guildford	Mitcham Junc.
03	Streatham Hill and Bognor Regis (special) ...	Norwood Junc., Redhill, Horsham and Littlehampton
04	London Bridge and Bognor Regis (special)	Streatham, Selhurst, West Croydon, Dorking North and Littlehampton
05	London Bridge and Coulsdon North	Forest Hill
06	Holborn, Wimbledon, Sutton and West Croydon	Herne Hill, Tulse Hill and St. Helier
06	Victoria and West Croydon	Streatham Hill and Crystal Palace
07	London Bridge and Littlehampton	Quarry and Horsham
08	Victoria (Eastern) and Sutton	Herne Hill, Wimbledon and St. Helier
08	Victoria and East Croydon	Streatham Common and Selhurst
09	London Bridge to London Bridge ...	Norwood Junc., Thornton Heath and Tulse Hill

Empty trains carry relevant numeral route indicator with a bar thereover except as shown below:—

2̄	London Bridge and Victoria	Denmark Hill
7̄	Victoria and London Bridge	Norwood Junc.
9̄	Victoria and New Cross Gate or London Bridge	Streatham Hill and Crystal Palace
2̄0̄	Tattenham Corner, Coulsdon North or East Croydon and Streatham Hill ...	Crystal Palace
3̄0̄	Victoria and West Croydon or Wallington ...	Streatham Common
3̄2̄	Victoria and Selhurst	Streatham Common
3̄4̄	Lancing to Durnsford Road	Ford
3̄6̄	Victoria and Beckenham Junc.	
3̄9̄	Streatham Hill to Epsom Downs	Norwood Junc. and West Croydon
4̄8̄	Gillingham and Streatham Hill	Beckenham Junc. and Crystal Palace
5̄1̄	Victoria and New Cross Gate or London Bridge	Streatham Hill and Crystal Palace
5̄6̄	Wimbledon to Victoria	Tooting
7̄1̄	Streatham Hill and Horsham	Norwood Junc.
9̄4̄	Victoria and Coulsdon North	Streatham Common
9̄7̄	Crawley and Horsham	

47

01	Victoria and Streatham Hill	
01	London Bridge and Streatham Hill	Tulse Hill
02	Victoria (Eastern) and Streatham Hill ...	Herne Hill and Tulse Hill
02	London Bridge and Peckham Rye	
02	Charing Cross and Cannon Street to New Cross Gate	
02	New Cross Gate to Charing Cross	
02	Streatham Common and Crystal Palace ...	Norwood Junc.
03	Holborn Viaduct and Streatham Hill	Herne Hill and Tulse Hill
04	Brighton, Lovers Walk to Durnsford Road ...	All routes
04	New Cross Gate and Cannon Street	
04	Selhurst Depot or Peckham Rye and Brighton, Lovers Walk or Lancing	All routes
04	Littlehampton, West Worthing, Lancing, Hove and Brighton (direct), or Lovers Walk via Preston Park	
06	Victoria and Crystal Palace or Wallington ...	Streatham Hill
06	London Bridge and New Cross Gate	
08	London Bridge and Streatham Hill	Forest Hill and Crystal Palace

EASTERN SECTION

The route via Sidcup is also known as the Dartford Loop Line

0	Maidstone East and Ashford	
0	Strood and Gillingham	
0	Elmers End and Hayes	
1	Strood and Maidstone West	
1	Grove Park and Bromley North	
1	Crowhurst and Bexhill West	
1	Sittingbourne and Sheerness	
1	St. Leonards and Hastings	
1	Ashford and Margate (not attached or detached at Ashford)	Canterbury West
2	Elmers End and Addiscombe	
2	Ashford and New Romney	
3	Elmers End and Sanderstead	
3	Holborn and Ramsgate	London Bridge, Greenwich and Chatham
4	Charing Cross and Margate	Orpington and Dover Priory
5	Cannon Street and Margate	Orpington and Dover Priory
6	Charing Cross and Margate	Swanley, Maidstone East and Dover Priory
7	Cannon Street and Margate	Swanley, Maidstone East and Dover Priory

9	Cannon Street and Bromley North	Parks Bridge
10	Charing Cross and Bromley North	Parks Bridge
12	Charing Cross and Orpington	Parks Bridge and Chislehurst
13	Cannon Street and Orpington	Parks Bridge and Chislehurst
14	Charing Cross and Orpington	Lewisham and Chislehurst
15	Cannon Street and Orpington	Lewisham and Chislehurst
16	Charing Cross and Sevenoaks	Parks Bridge and Orpington
17	Cannon Street or Holborn to Sevenoaks ...	London Bridge, Parks Bridge and Orpington
17	Sevenoaks to Cannon Street or London Bridge	Parks Bridge
18	Charing Cross and Sevenoaks	Lewisham and Orpington
18	Charing Cross and Margate	Orpington, Dover Priory and Minster
19	Cannon Street and Sevenoaks	Lewisham and Orpington
19	Cannon Street and Margate	Orpington, Dover Priory
20	Ashford and Hastings	
20	Charing Cross and Beckenham Junc.	Lewisham
21	Holborn or Blackfriars and London Bridge ...	Herne Hill, Tulse Hill St. Helier and West Croydon
21	Cannon Street and Beckenham Junc.	Lewisham
22	Charing Cross and Hastings	Orpington and Battle
23	Holborn and Bickley	Herne Hill
23	Tonbridge and Hastings	
23	Cannon Street and Dover Priory	Greenwich, Woolwich Arsenal and Chatham
24	Tonbridge and Bexhill West	
24	Charing Cross and Hayes	Lewisham
24	Victoria and Bickley	Herne Hill
25	Cannon Street and Hayes	Lewisham
25	Blackfriars and Bickley	Herne Hill
26	Charing Cross and Addiscombe	Lewisham
26	Victoria and Bickley	Catford Loop
27	Cannon Street and Addiscombe	Lewisham
27	Holborn and Bickley	Catford Loop
28	Charing Cross and Sanderstead or Selsdon ...	Lewisham
29	Cannon Street and Sanderstead or Selsdon ...	Lewisham
29	Blackfriars and Bickley	Catford Loop
30	Charing Cross and Beckenham Junc.	Parks Bridge
30	Victoria and Dover Priory	Herne Hill and Chatham

31	Victoria and Dover Priory	Catford Loop and Chatham
31	Cannon Street and Beckenham Junc.	Parks Bridge
32	Charing Cross and Dover Priory	Swanley and Chatham
33	Cannon Street and Hastings	Orpington and Battle
34	Holborn and Ramsgate	Herne Hill and Chatham
34	Charing Cross and Hayes	Parks Bridge
35	Cannon Street and Hayes	Parks Bridge
35	Holborn and Ramsgate	Catford Loop and Chatham
36	Holborn and Sheerness	Herne Hill and Sittingbourne
36	Charing Cross and Addiscombe	Parks Bridge
37	Cannon Street and Addiscombe	Parks Bridge
37	Holborn and Sheerness	Catford Loop and Sittingbourne
38	Charing Cross and Sanderstead or Selsdon ...	Parks Bridge
39	Cannon Street and Sanderstead or Selsdon ...	Parks Bridge
39	Gillingham or Fawkham to Blackfriars	Catford Loop
40	Charing Cross and Dartford	Parks Bridge and Sidcup
40	Victoria and Margate	Herne Hill and Chatham
41	Victoria and Margate	Catford Loop and Chatham
41	Cannon Street and Dartford	Parks Bridge and Sidcup
42	Charing Cross and Gillingham or Ramsgate ...	Parks Bridge and Sidcup
43	Cannon Street and Gillingham or Ramsgate	Parks Bridge and Sidcup
44	Charing Cross and New Romney	Orpington and Ashford
45	Orpington to Holborn	Parks Bridge and London Bridge
46	Charing Cross and Gravesend or Maidstone West	Parks Bridge and Sidcup
47	Cannon Street and Gravesend or Maidstone West	Parks Bridge and Sidcup
48	Holborn or Blackfriars and Bromley North ...	London Bridge
49	Holborn or Blackfriars and Dartford or Gravesend	London Bridge, Parks Bridge and Sidcup
50	Charing Cross and Dartford	Lewisham and Sidcup
50	Victoria and Ramsgate	Herne Hill and Chatham
51	Victoria and Ramsgate	Catford Loop and Chatham
51	Cannon Street and Dartford	Lewisham and Sidcup

52	Charing Cross and Gillingham	Lewisham and Sidcup
53	Cannon Street and Gillingham	Lewisham and Sidcup
54	Herne Hill and Ramsgate	Chatham
56	Charing Cross and Gravesend or Maidstone West	Lewisham and Sidcup
57	Cannon Street and Gravesend or Maidstone West	Lewisham and Sidcup
58	Holborn or Blackfriars and Gillingham ...	Nunhead, Lewisham and Sidcup
59	Holborn or Blackfriars to Gillingham	London Bridge, Lewisham and Sidcup
60	Charing Cross and Dartford	Blackheath and Charlton
60	Victoria and Sheerness	Herne Hill and Sittingbourne
61	Blackfriars and Orpington or Sevenoaks ...	Herne Hill and Petts Wood
61	Ashford and Margate	Dover Priory
62	Charing Cross and Gillingham or Ramsgate ...	Blackheath and Charlton
63	Cannon Street and Gillingham or Ramsgate ...	Blackheath and Charlton
63	Blackfriars and Orpington or Sevenoaks ...	Catford Loop and Petts Wood
64	Victoria and Sheerness	Catford Loop and Sittingbourne
64	Charing Cross and Gravesend or Maidstone West	Blackheath and Charlton
65	Cannon Street and Gravesend or Maidstone West	Blackheath and Charlton
65	Blackfriars and Swanley or Sevenoaks	Herne Hill
66	Charing Cross and Hastings	Orpington and Ashford
67	Blackfriars and Swanley or Sevenoaks ...	Catford Loop
68	Charing Cross and Margate	Chislehurst, Swanley, Sevenoaks and Dover Priory
68	Holborn or Blackfriars and Dartford or Gravesend	Nunhead and Blackheath
69	Holborn or Blackfriars and Dartford or Gravesend	London Bridge, Blackheath and Charlton
70	Charing Cross and Dartford	Bexleyheath
70	Victoria and Orpington or Sevenoaks	Herne Hill and Petts Wood
71	Cannon Street and Dartford	Bexleyheath
71	Holborn and Orpington or Sevenoaks ...	Herne Hill and Petts Wood

72	Victoria and Orpington or Sevenoaks	Catford Loop and Petts Wood
72	Charing Cross and Gillingham or Ramsgate	Bexleyheath
73	Cannon Street and Gillingham or Ramsgate ...	Bexleyheath
73	Holborn and Orpington or Sevenoaks	Catford Loop Petts Wood
74	Charing Cross and Gravesend or Maidstone West	Bexleyheath
74	Victoria and Dover Marine	Herne Hill and Chatham
75	Victoria and Dover Marine	Catford Loop and Chatham
75	Cannon Street and Gravesend or Maidstone West	Bexleyheath
75	Holborn or Blackfriars and Herne Hill ...	
76	London Bridge (L.L.) and Gravesend ...	Bexleyheath
76	Victoria and Herne Hill	
76	Holborn or Blackfriars and Cannon Street ...	
77	Cannon Street and Hastings	Orpington and Ashford
78	Charing Cross and Margate	Chislehurst, Swanley, Sevenoaks and Canterbury West
78	Holborn or Blackfriars to Dartford or Gravesend	Nunhead and Bexleyheath
78	Gravesend or Dartford to Blackfriars	Bexleyheath and Nunhead
79	Gravesend or Dartford to Holborn	Bexleyheath and Nunhead
79	Holborn or Blackfriars to Dartford or Gravesend	London Bridge and Bexleyheath
80	Charing Cross and Dartford	Greenwich
80	Victoria and Swanley or Sevenoaks	Herne Hill
80	Strood and Dover Priory	
81	Cannon Street and Dartford	Greenwich
81	Holborn and Swanley or Sevenoaks	Herne Hill
81	Strood and Ramsgate	
82	Charing Cross and Gillingham or Ramsgate	Greenwich
82	Victoria and Swanley or Sevenoaks	Catford Loop
83	Cannon Street and Gillingham or Ramsgate	Greenwich
83	Holborn and Swanley or Sevenoaks	Catford Loop
84	Sheerness and Dover Priory	
84	Charing Cross to Paddock Wood	Greenwich, Strood and Maidstone West
85	Cannon Street and Gravesend or Maidstone West	Greenwich
85	Sheerness and Ramsgate	
85	Holborn or Blackfriars to Orpington ...	Nunhead, Lewisham and Beckenham Junc.

85	Orpington to Holborn	Beckenham Junc., Lewisham and Nunhead
86	Charing Cross and Margate	Chislehurst, Swanley, Maidstone East and Canterbury West
87	Cannon Street and Margate	Chislehurst, Swanley, Maidstone East and Canterbury West
88	Charing Cross and New Romney	Swanley and Maidstone East
89	Holborn or Blackfriars and Dartford or Gravesend	London Bridge and Greenwich
90	Victoria and Sheerness	Herne Hill and Western Junc.
90	Charing Cross and Margate	Orpington and Canterbury West
91	Holborn and Sheerness	Herne Hill and Western Junc.
91	Cannon Street and Margate	Orpington and Canterbury West
92	Victoria and Sheerness	Catford Loop and Western Junc.
93	Holborn and Sheerness	Catford Loop and Western Junc.
93	Charing Cross or Cannon Street to Caterham	
93	Tattenham Corner or Caterham to Cannon Street	
94	Victoria and Maidstone East	Herne Hill
94	Charing Cross and Sheerness	Greenwich and Western Junc.
95	Holborn and Maidstone East	Herne Hill
95	Cannon Street and Sheerness	Greenwich and Western Junc.
96	Victoria and Maidstone East	Catford Loop
96	Charing Cross and Sheerness	Greenwich and Sittingbourne
97	Holborn and Maidstone East	Catford Loop
97	Cannon Street and Sheerness	Greenwich and Sittingbourne
97	Charing Cross and Reigate	
01	Charing Cross or Cannon Street to Tattenham Corner	
01	Tattenham Corner or Caterham to Charing Cross	
02	Victoria and Streatham Hill	Herne Hill
03	Holborn Viaduct and Streatham Hill	Herne Hill
03	Cannon Street and Dover Priory	Swanley and Chatham
05	Cannon Street and Sevenoaks	Chislehurst and Swanley

06	Charing Cross and Sevenoaks	Chislehurst and Swanley
07	Cannon Street and Gillingham or Ramsgate	Swanley and Chatham
08	Charing Cross and Gillingham or Ramsgate	Swanley and Chatham
08	Victoria (Eastern) and Sutton	Herne Hill, Wimbledon and St. Helier
09	Cannon Street and Maidstone East	Chislehurst and Swanley

Empty trains carry relevant numeral route indicator with a bar thereover except as shown below

$\bar{2}$	Charing Cross and Cannon Street	
$\bar{5}$	Cannon Street and Blackheath	Ludgate Hill
$\bar{9}$	Cannon Street to Grove Park	
$\overline{10}$	Charing Cross to Grove Park	
$\overline{16}$	Stewarts Lane and Ramsgate	Herne Hill and Chatham
$\overline{16}$	Dover Marine to Stewarts Lane	Chatham and Herne Hill
$\overline{17}$	Stewarts Lane and Ramsgate	Catford Loop and Chatham
$\overline{17}$	Dover Marine to Stewarts Lane	Chatham and Catford Loop
$\overline{22}$	Charing Cross to Grove Park	
$\overline{22}$	Blackheath or Grove Park to Charing Cross	
$\overline{33}$	Cannon Street to Grove Park	
$\overline{33}$	Blackheath or Grove Park to Cannon Street	
$\overline{38}$	Holborn and Grove Park	Nunhead
$\overline{38}$	Grove Park to Cannon Street	Nunhead
$\overline{48}$	Streatham Hill and Gillingham	Crystal Palace and Beckenham Junc.
$\overline{60}$	Charing Cross to Blackheath	
$\overline{61}$	Cannon Street to Blackheath	
$\overline{66}$	Charing Cross to Rotherhithe Road	
$\overline{68}$	Blackheath to Holborn or Cannon Street	Ludgate Hill
$\overline{76}$	Cannon Street to Stewarts Lane or Victoria	Blackheath and Ludgate Hill
$\overline{77}$	Cannon Street to Rotherhithe Road	
$\overline{79}$	Victoria and Streatham	Stewarts Lane Junc.
$\overline{01}$	Victoria and Grove Park	Nunhead
$\overline{01}$	St. Leonards (W.M.) and Hastings	
$\overline{02}$	Charing Cross or Cannon Street to New Cross Gate	
$\overline{02}$	New Cross Gate to Charing Cross	
$\overline{02}$	St. Leonards and Bexhill West	Crowhurst

03	Victoria to Stewarts Lane	
04	New Cross Gate to Cannon Street	
04	Stewarts Lane and Grove Park	Nunhead
05	Holborn and Stewarts Lane	
05	Stewarts Lane to Cannon Street	Blackfriars or Ludgate Hill
06	St. Leonards and Folkestone Junc.	
07	Victoria and Holborn	
07	Victoria to Cannon Street	Blackfriars or Ludgate Hill
07	St. Leonards and Deal	Ashford and Minster
08	St. Leonards and Deal	Ashford and Dover Priory
09	Blackheath and Stewarts Lane	Nunhead

Eastern Section "Boat Train" Headcodes

12	Victoria and Dover Marine	Herne Hill and Maidstone East
13	Victoria and Dover Marine	Catford and Maidstone East
14	Victoria and Dover Marine or Folkestone Harbour	Herne Hill, Swanley and Sevenoaks
15	Victoria and Dover Marine or Folkestone Harbour	Catford, Swanley and Sevenoaks
42	Victoria and Folkestone Harbour	Herne Hill and Maidstone East
43	Victoria and Folkestone Harbour	Catford and Maidstone East
46	Victoria and Dover Marine	Herne Hill and Orpington
47	Victoria and Dover Marine	Catford and Orpington
56	Victoria and Folkestone Harbour	Herne Hill and Orpington
57	Victoria and Folkestone Harbour	Catford and Orpington

Eastern Section Freight Headcodes

On the introduction in 1960 of their Type 3 diesel-electrics, for freight haulage, the Southern Region commenced a new series of two-character headcodes, for use not only on the new diesels but also on the existing 2,500 h.p. electric locomotives. The indicator panel is situated centrally on the cab front, between the two driving windows. The code indicates routes; no attempt is made to number individual trains. Many combinations are not listed here; trains carrying such codes are specials, to which code numbers are allocated at short notice.

Code		Route
AA	Southwark Depot or Hither Green sidings and Dover Marine (or stations short thereof)	Swanley and Chatham
AB	Southwark Depot or Hither Green sidings and Dover Marine (or stations short thereof)	Orpington
AC	Southwark Depot or Hither Green sidings and Dover Marine (or stations short thereof)	Maidstone East
AD	Southwark Depot and Bricklayers' Arms ...	
AE	Bricklayers' Arms and Dover Marine (or stations short thereof)	Maidstone East
AF	Bricklayers' Arms and Dover Marine (or stations short thereof)	Orpington
AG	St. Johns and Dover Marine (or stations short thereof)	Maidstone East
AH	St. Johns and Dover Marine (or stations short thereof)	Orpington
AJ	Faversham and Dover Marine	
AK	Folkestone Junc. and Dover Marine	
BA	Hither Green sidings and Willesden ...	Nunhead and West London line
BB	Hither Green sidings and Old Oak Common	Nunhead and West London line
BC	Hither Green sidings and Feltham	Nunhead and West London line
BD	Plumstead and Willesden	Blackheath, Nunhead and West London line
BE	Plumstead and Old Oak Common	Blackheath, Nunhead and West London line
BF	Plumstead and Feltham	Blackheath, Nunhead and West London line
BG	Bricklayers' Arms and Willesden	Blackheath, Nunhead and West London line
BH	Blackheath and Willesden	Nunhead and West London line
BJ	Hoo Junction and Willesden	Crayford, Nunhead and West London line
BK	Hoo Junction and Willesden	Plumstead, Nunhead and West London line

0A	Bricklayers' Arms and Dover Town (or stations short thereof)	Orpington
1A	Bricklayers' Arms and Dover Town (or stations short thereof)	Maidstone East
2A	Bricklayers' Arms and Dover Town (or stations short thereof)	Swanley and Chatham
3A	Bricklayers' Arms and Dover Town (or stations short thereof)	Crayford and Chatham
4A	Bricklayers' Arms and Ramsgate	Swanley and Chatham
5A	Bricklayers' Arms and Maidstone West ...	Orpington
6A	Bricklayers' Arms and Queenborough ...	Crayford and Chatham
7A	Bricklayers' Arms and Hastings	Orpington and Tonbridge
8A	Bricklayers' Arms (or intermediate stations) and Dartford (or stations short thereof)	Lewisham and Plumstead
9A	Bricklayers' Arms and Dartford (or stations short thereof)	Crayford
0B	Bricklayers' Arms and Hither Green sidings	Lewisham
1B	Bricklayers' Arms and Hither Green sidings	Parks Bridge Junc.
2B	Bricklayers' Arms (or intermediate stations) and Hayes (or stations short thereof) ...	Parks Bridge Junc.
3B	Bricklayers' Arms (or intermediate stations) and Beckenham Junction	Parks Bridge Junc.
4B	Bricklayers' Arms (or intermediate stations) and Addiscombe	Parks Bridge Junc.
5B	Bricklayers' Arms and Hayes	Parks Bridge Junc., Addiscombe and Elmers End
6B	Bricklayers' Arms and Blackfriars	London Bridge
0C	Herne Hill sidings and Dover Town (or stations short thereof)	Orpington
1C	Herne Hill sidings and Dover Town (or stations short thereof)	Maidstone East
2C	Herne Hill sidings and Dover Town (or stations short thereof)	Chatham
3C	Herne Hill sidings and Hoo Junction ...	Blackfriars, Nunhead and Crayford
4C	Herne Hill sidings and Hither Green sidings	Camberwell and Nunhead
5C	Herne Hill sidings and Hither Green sidings	Blackfriars and Nunhead
6C	Herne Hill sidings and Plumstead	Camberwell and Blackfriars
7C	Herne Hill sidings and Bellingham	Camberwell and Nunhead
8C	Herne Hill sidings and Brockley Lane ...	Camberwell and Nunhead
9C	Herne Hill and Blackfriars	
0D	Herne Hill sidings (or intermediate stations) and Sevenoaks (or stations short thereof)	Beckenham Junc. and Orpington
1D	Herne Hill sidings and Stewarts Lane ...	Herne Hill

8D	Ashford (or intermediate stations) and Bexhill Central (or stations short thereof)	
9D	Ashford (or intermediate stations) and New Romney (or stations short thereof) ...	
0E	Hither Green sidings and Dover Town (or stations short thereof)	Orpington
1E	Hither Green sidings and Dover Town (or stations short thereof)	Maidstone East
2E	Hither Green sidings and Dover Town (or stations short thereof)	Swanley and Chatham
3E	Hither Green sidings and Dover Town ...	Crayford and Chatham
4E	Hither Green sidings (or intermediate stations) and Hoo Junction (or stations short thereof)	Crayford
5E	Hither Green sidings and Maidstone West	Crayford
6E	Hither Green sidings and Angerstein Wharf (or stations short thereof)	Crayford spur
7E	Hither Green sidings and Hastings	Orpington and Tonbridge
8E	Hither Green sidings and Plumstead ...	Brockley Lane
9E	Hither Green sidings and St. Mary Cray ...	
0F	Hither Green sidings and Blackheath ...	St. Johns
1F	Hither Green sidings and Blackheath ...	Brockley Lane
2F	Hither Green sidings (or intermediate stations) and Blackheath (or stations short thereof)	Crayford and Bexleyheath
3F	Hither Green sidings and Bromley North	
4F	Hither Green sidings and Blackfriars ...	Nunhead
5F	Hither Green sidings and Blackfriars ...	London Bridge
6F	Hither Green sidings and Gravesend West	
0G	Tonbridge West Yard (or intermediate stations) and Dover Town (or stations short thereof)	
1G	Tonbridge West Yard and Angerstein Wharf	Maidstone West and Plumstead
2G	Tonbridge West Yard and Minster	Ashford
3G	Tonbridge West Yard (or intermediate stations) and Swanley (or stations short thereof)	
5G	Tonbridge West Yard (or intermediate stations) and Hoo Junction (or stations short thereof)	Maidstone West
6G	Tonbridge West Yard (or intermediate stations) and Bexhill West	
7G	Tonbridge West Yard (or intermediate stations) and Hastings (or stations short thereof)	
8G	Tonbridge West Yard (or intermediate stations) and Tunbridge Wells West ...	
0H	Hoo Junction (or intermediate stations) and Queenborough	Chatham

1H	Hoo Junction and Dover Town		Chatham, Queenborough and Selling
2H	Hoo Junction (or intermediate stations) and Dover Town (or stations short thereof)		Chatham and Selling
3H	Hoo Junction and Dover Town		Chatham, Ramsgate and Deal
4H	Hoo Junction and Angerstein Wharf ...		Dartford
5H	Hoo Junction and Plumstead		Dartford
0J	Faversham and Ramsgate (or stations short thereof)		
1J	Faversham and Deal		Ramsgate
2J	Faversham and Sittingbourne (or stations short thereof)		Queenborough
3J	Faversham and Shorncliffe		Canterbury East and Dover
4J	Faversham (or intermediate stations) and Swanley (or stations short thereof) ...		
0K	Ashford and Ashford		Dover and Minster
1K	Blackheath (or intermediate stations) and Plumstead (or stations short thereof) ...		Bexleyheath
2K	Dover Town (or intermediate stations) and Ashford (or stations short thereof) ...		Minster
3K	Dover Town and Ramsgate		
4K	Farningham Road (or intermediate stations) and Gravesend West (or stations short thereof)		
5K	Margate (or intermediate stations) and Ashford (or stations short thereof) ...		Minster
6K	Sheerness-on-Sea and Queenborough ...		
7K	Snodland and Snowdown Colliery sidings ...		Strood
8K	Snowdown Colliery sidings and Sittingbourne (or stations short thereof)		Queenborough

LONDON MIDLAND REGION

Although the four-character code is increasingly used, two-character codes still predominate in all parts of the London Midland Region, particularly the Lancashire area. The codes listed below are gradually becoming obsolete as units fitted to display two characters are modified to display four. The first character is a letter indicating the class (see page 21). The second, listed here, is a figure indicating the service.

London Midland Route Codes
LONDON AREA

Down	Up	Service
1	1	Euston and Watford
2	2	Broad Street and Watford
3	3	Watford and St. Albans

Down	Up	Service
3	3	Harrow & Wealdstone and Belmont
4	4	Broad Street or Willesden (High Level) to Richmond
5	4	Broad Street and Willesden (High Level)
6	1	Euston and Willesden (New Station)
6	2	Broad Street and Willesden (New Station)
7	1	Euston and Harrow & Wealdstone
7	2	Broad Street and Harrow & Wealdstone
8	1	Euston and Bushey & Oxhey
8	2	Broad Street and Bushey & Oxhey
9	1	Euston and Croxley Green
9	2	Broad Street and Croxley Green
9	9	Watford Junc. and Croxley Green
0	0	Empty trains to Mitre Bridge carriage sidings
—	7	Watford Junc. and Harrow & Wealdstone
X	X	Empty trains to Dalston sidings
Y	Y	Empty trains to Croxley Green carriage sidings
Z	Z	Empty trains to Stonebridge Park carriage sidings

WESTERN SECTION

Down	Up	Service
1	1	Bletchley and Banbury
1	1	Birmingham and Stafford or intermediate stations via Dudley Port and Wolverhampton
1	1	Rugby and Stafford via Birmingham and Dudley Port
1	1	Birmingham and Coventry, Rugby or Northampton
2	2	Bletchley and Wolverton or Oxford
2	2	Dudley and Walsall
2	2	Birmingham and Lichfield or Burton via Four Oaks
2	2	Nuneaton and Coventry or Leamington
2	2	Rugby and Leicester
2	2	Northampton and Bedford
3	3	Bletchley and Bedford or Cambridge
3	3	Birmingham and Wolverhampton or Stafford via Soho East Junc. and Bescot
3	3	Birmingham and Walsall via Streetly
3	3	Rugby and Peterborough
4	4	Birmingham and Rugeley or Stafford via Soho East Junc. and Walsall
6	6	Birmingham and Lichfield via Aston and Walsall
6	6	Nuneaton and Rugby or Stafford
7	7	Birmingham and Leamington via Berkswell
7	7	Wolverhampton and Lichfield or Burton via Walsall
8	8	Birmingham and Leamington via Coventry
8	8	Wolverhampton and Rugeley or Stafford via Walsall
9	9	Birmingham and Wolverhampton or Stafford via Aston and Bescot
9	9	Birmingham and Rugeley or Stafford via Aston and Bescot
0	0	Birmingham and Monument Lane via Aston
0	0	Wolverhampton and Sutton Park via Walsall

MIDLAND SECTION

Down	Up	Service
1	1	Bedford and Hitchin
1	1	Derby and Lincoln via Nottingham
1	1	Rugby and Peterborough
1	1	St. Pancras and St. Albans (for two-character fitted vehicles only)
2	2	Bedford and Northampton

Down	Up	Service
2	2	Leicester and Rugby
2	2	St. Pancras and Harpenden (for two-character fitted vehicles only)
2	2	Burton and Birmingham via Lichfield and Four Oaks
3	3	Derby and Leicester via Burton
3	3	St. Pancras and Luton (for two-character fitted vehicles only)
3	3	Birmingham and Walsall via Sutton Park
4	4	Nottingham and Leicester
4	4	St. Pancras to Bedford (for two-character fitted vehicles only)
5	5	Leicester and Nuneaton
5	5	St. Pancras and Kettering (for two-character fitted vehicles only)
5	5	Birmingham and Evesham via Church Road Junction
6	6	Derby and Crewe
6	6	Nottingham and Melton Mowbray
6	6	St. Pancras and Barking (for two-character fitted vehicles only)
6	6	Birmingham and Evesham via Camp Hill
7	7	Bedford and Kettering
7	7	Nottingham and Birmingham via Leicester and Nuneaton
7	7	Burton and Walsall or Wolverhampton via Lichfield
7	7	Leicester and Buxton or Miller's Dale
8	8	Derby and Birmingham or King's Norton via Whitacre
8	8	Kettering and Wellingborough
9	9	Bedford and Luton
9	9	Derby and Birmingham or King's Norton via Kingsbury
9	9	Leicester and Kettering
0	0	Leicester and Sutton Park or Wolverhampton via Walsall

NORTH WALES DISTRICT

Down	Up	Service
1	1	Bangor and Rhyl
2	4	Llandudno and Rhyl
2	2	Llandudno and Blaenau Festiniog (North)
2	2	Chester and Shotton or Wrexham Central
3	3	Llandudno and Pwllheli via Bangor and Afon Wen
3	5	Amlwch and Llandudno
3	5	New Brighton or Neston and Chester
4	2	Rhyl and Llandudno
4	4	New Brighton and Wrexham (Central)
5	3	Llandudno and Amlwch
5	3	Chester (Northgate) and Neston or New Brighton
5	5	Crewe and Shrewsbury
6	6	Llandudno and Crewe
7	7	Rhyl and Blaenau Festiniog (North)

LANCASHIRE AREA

Down	Up	Service
0	0	Manchester (Victoria) and Colne or intermediate stations via Bolton and Blackburn
0	0	Manchester (Victoria) and Middleton
0	0	Kenyon Junc. and Allerton Depot
0	0	Manchester (Oxford Road) and Manchester (Piccadilly)
0	2	The Crewe line and Manchester (Oxford Road) via Stockport
0	3	Buxton and Manchester (Oxford Road)

Down	Up	Service
0	4	Stafford and Manchester (Oxford Road) or intermediate stations via Stoke-on-Trent, Kidsgrove and Cheadle Hulme
0	5	Cresswell or Uttoxeter and Manchester (Oxford Road) via Stoke-on-Trent, Kidsgrove and Cheadle Hulme
0	5	Rochdale and Blackburn via Bury
1	1	Liverpool (Lime Street) and Leeds (City) or intermediate stations via Huddersfield
1	1	Manchester (Piccadilly) and Wilmslow or Crewe line
1	1	Liverpool (Central) and Warrington (Central) via Widnes (North)
1	2	Skipton or Todmorden and Blackpool (Central) or intermediate stations via Blackburn and Farington Curve Junc.
1	5	Rochdale and Blackpool (Central) via Bury
1	7	Wilmslow or the Crewe line via Styal
1	8	Manchester (Victoria) and Blackpool (Central) via Bolton
2	2	Skipton or Todmorden and Blackpool (Central) or intermediate stations via Blackburn and Todd Lane Junc.
2	2	Manchester (Victoria) and Bury or Bacup or intermediate stations via Heywood
2	2	Manchester (Piccadilly) and the Crewe line via Stockport
2	2	Liverpool (Lime Street) and Wigan (North Western)
2	2	Liverpool (Central) and Warrington via Widnes
2	0	Crewe line and Manchester (Oxford Road) via Stockport
2	1/3/8	Blackpool or Fleetwood and Skipton, or intermediate stations via Blackburn
2	4	Southport and Blackpool (Central) or intermediate stations
2	6	Manchester (Victoria) and Blackpool (Central) via Atherton
3	3	Manchester (Piccadilly) and Buxton
3	3	Manchester (Victoria) and Royton
3	3	Manchester (Central) and Chester, or intermediate stations
3	3	Liverpool (Central) and Aintree (Central) or Gateacre
3	3	Liverpool (Lime Street) and Crewe
3	0	Manchester, Oxford Road and Buxton
3	2	Skipton or Todmorden and Blackpool (North) or Fleetwood, or intermediate stations, via Blackburn and Farington Curve Junc.
3	4	Southport and Blackpool (North) or Fleetwood
3	5	Rochdale and Blackpool (North) via Bury
3	8	Manchester (Victoria) and Blackpool (North) via Bolton
4	4	Manchester (Piccadilly) and Stafford, or intermediate stations via Cheadle Hulme, Kidsgrove and Stoke-on-Trent
4	4	Manchester (Victoria) and Oldham or Rochdale via Hollinwood or Middleton Junc.
4	4	Liverpool (Central) and Allerton sidings
4	0	Manchester (Oxford Road) and Stafford via Cheadle Hulme, Kidsgrove and Stoke-on-Trent
4	2/3	Blackpool or Fleetwood and Southport via Crossens or Burscough Bridge
4	6	Manchester (Victoria) and Southport via Atherton
4	9	Skipton or Todmorden and Southport or intermediate stations via Crossens or Burscough Bridge and Blackburn
5	5	Liverpool (Exchange) and Rochdale or intermediate stations via Bolton and Bury
5	5	Liverpool (Lime Street) and Chester
5	5	Manchester (Piccadilly) and Cresswell or Uttoxeter via Cheadle Hulme, Kidsgrove and Stoke-on-Trent
5	5	Manchester (Central) and Warrington (Central)
5	0	Manchester (Oxford Road) and Cresswell or Uttoxeter via Cheadle Hulme, Kidsgrove and Stoke-on-Trent
5	0	Blackburn and Rochdale via Bury

Down	Up	Service
5	1	Blackpool (Central) and Rochdale via Bury
5	2	Bacup and Rochdale via Bury
5	3	Blackpool (North) or Fleetwood and Rochdale via Bury
5	8	Skipton and Barnoldswick
5	8	Manchester (Victoria) and Liverpool (Exchange) via Bolton
5	9	Southport and Rochdale via Bury
6	6	Manchester (Victoria) and Stockport or Stalybridge
6	6	Manchester (Victoria) and Crewe or Derby (Midland)
6	6	Manchester (Victoria) and Liverpool (Exchange) via Atherton
6	6	Manchester (Victoria) and Rochdale or Todmorden via Castleton
6	6	Liverpool (Central) and Manchester (Central)
6	6	St. Helens and Warrington (Bank Quay)
6	6	Warrington (Bank Quay) and Acton Bridge
6	2	Blackpool (Central) and Manchester (Victoria) via Atherton
6	4	Southport and Manchester (Victoria) via Atherton
6	8	Blackpool (North) or Fleetwood and Manchester (Victoria) via Atherton
7	7	Manchester (Victoria) and Buxton or Miller's Dale
7	7	Manchester (Victoria) and Skipton or intermediate stations via Clifton Junc., Bury and Accrington
7	7	Blackpool (North) and Fleetwood via the Poulton Curve
7	7	Warrington (Bank Quay) and Kenyon Junc.
7	1	Manchester (Oxford Road) and Wilmslow or the Crewe line via Styal
8	8	Manchester (Oxford Road) and Liverpool (Lime Street)
8	2	Skipton or Todmorden or intermediate stations and Blackpool (North) or Fleetwood via Todd Lane Junc.
8	5	Barnoldswick and Skipton
8	—	All stations to Manchester (Victoria) via Bolton
9	9	Stockport or Tiviot Dale and Warrington (Central)
9	9	Allerton Depot and St. Helens
9	4	Southport and Skipton or Todmorden or intermediate stations via Crossens or Burscough Bridge

CARLISLE AREA

Down	Up	Service
1	1	Carlisle and Silloth
2	2	Carlisle and Whitehaven via Maryport
3	3	Carlisle and Whitehaven via Penrith
4	4	Carlisle and Dumfries

NORTH EASTERN REGION

Instead of introducing the standard four-character headcode system on its diesel multiple-units, the North Eastern Region retains its straightforward two-character code. The first character is a letter indicating the class of train, the second a figure indicating the actual route of the train. A list of route codes is given below. The diesel locomotives used on the North Eastern Region continue to display the standard disc code described on page 5.

The N.E.R. route codes are repeated in five different districts.

N.E.R. Route Codes

TEES-SIDE DISTRICT

Route No.
1. Darlington—Saltburn line
2. Darlington—Crook line
3. { Darlington—Barnard Castle
    Darlington—Penrith
    Middlesbrough—West Hartlepool—Newcastle
4. { Darlington—Middleton-in-Teesdale
    Bishop Auckland—Middleton-in-Teesdale
5. Bishop Auckland—Durham
6. { Middlesbrough—Whitby—Scarborough
    Billingham—Haverton Hill
7. { Middlesbrough—Northallerton
    Darlington—Richmond
8. Middlesbrough—Guisborough
9. Darlington—Leeds

NEWCASTLE-ON-TYNE DISTRICT

Route No.
1. Newcastle—Hexham—Carlisle via Blaydon
2. Newcastle—Hexham—Carlisle via Lemington
3. Newcastle—Middlesbrough
4. Newcastle—Sunderland—West Hartlepool
5. Sunderland—Durham—Bishop Auckland
6. Sunderland—South Shields
7. Blyth—Tyne
8. Newcastle—Alnmouth—Alnwick
9. Main line trains

HULL AND YORK DISTRICTS

Route No.
0. Selby—Goole
1. Hull and Doncaster or beyond, includes Thorne North, Stainforth and Sheffield (Victoria) or Sheffield (Midland)
2. Hull—Leeds
3. { Selby—Driffield—Bridlington
    Hull—Withernsea*
4. { Hull—Scarborough
    Hull—York via Church Fenton†
5. Hull—York via Market Weighton
6. Hull—Hornsea
7. Hull—Goole—Snaith—Wakefield
8. Hull—Brough
9. Hull—Beverley

*The same code is used for both these branches, since they do not conflict with each other

†The only service between Hull and York via Church Fenton is on Sundays, when there is no service on the Scarborough line in summer. There is therefore no risk of confliction.

WAKEFIELD DISTRICT

Route No.

0
- Leeds City—Knottingly via Castleford (Cutsdyke)
- Bradford (Hammerton Street)—Bradford (Forster Square) via the Quarry Gap

1 Bradford (Exchange)—Harrogate via Stanningley
2 Bradford (Exchange)—Harrogate via Pudsey
3 Bradford (Exchange)—Leeds (Central) via Stanningley
4 Bradford (Exchange)—Leeds (Central) via Pudsey

5
- Wakefield (Westgate)—Huddersfield
- Bradford (Exchange)—Penistone via Halifax

6
- Bradford (Exchange)—Penistone via Cleckheaton branch
- Leeds (Central)—Doncaster (Central)

7 Bradford (Exchange)—Wakefield, Goole and Hull

8
- Bradford (Exchange)—Clayton West via Halifax
- Leeds (Central)—Castleford (Central)—Knottingley
- Leeds (City)—Barnsley (Exchange)—Sheffield (Midland) via Wakefield (Kirkgate)

9
- Bradford (Exchange)—Clayton West via Cleckheaton branch
- Bradford (Hammerton Street)—Leeds (City)

LEEDS DISTRICT

Route Nos.
Down Up

0 { 0
- Leeds—Knottingley via Methley Junc.
- Bradford (Forster Square)—Bradford (Hammerton Street) via Shipley (Windhill)

1 { 1
- Leeds—Skipton via Keighley
- Leeds—Manchester—Liverpool via Mirfield and Dewsbury

2 { 2
- Leeds—Bradford (Forster Square)
- Leeds (City)—Hull
- Leeds—Huddersfield via Spen Valley line

3 {
- 3 Leeds—Skipton via Guisley and Ilkley
- 5 Huddersfield—Penistone
- 8 Huddersfield—Clayton West
- 3 Huddersfield—Brockholes

4 { 4
- Leeds—Skipton via Otley and Ilkley
- Penistone—Huddersfield—Wakefield (West)

5 { 5
- Bradford (Forster Square)—Skipton via Keighley
- Leeds (City)—Harrogate via Wetherby
- Bradford (Exchange)—Penistone via Halifax and Huddersfield
- 0 Bradford (Exchange)—Huddersfield only, via Halifax

6 { 6
- Bradford (Forster Square)—Skipton via Ilkley
- Leeds (City)—York
- Leeds—Sheffield
- Bradford (Exchange) — Penistone via Cleckheaton and Huddersfield
- 0 Bradford (Exchange)—Huddersfield only, via Cleckheaton

7 7 Leeds (City)—Harrogate—Northallerton

8 { 8
- Leeds—Barnsley via Wakefield (Kirkgate)
- Castleford—Leeds (Central)—Ilkley
- Bradford (Exchange)—Huddersfield—Clayton West via Halifax

9 { 9
- Bradford (Exchange) — Huddersfield — Clayton West via Cleckheaton
- Leeds (City)/Leeds (Central)—Bradford (Hammerton Street)

SCOTTISH REGION

The Scottish Region, like the North Eastern, has decided to use a two-character code, in preference to the four-character code, on its internal services. At present, however, only the Glasgow electric trains are fitted to display it; all other units throughout the Region carry the standard headlamp code. The Glasgow two-character code consists of two figures, the first indicating destination and the second the description and route.

Scottish Region Two-Character Code

First Fig.   **Destination**
1. Helensburgh (Central) or Airdrie
2. Balloch or Bridgeton (Central)
3. Dalmuir Park
4. Clydebank (Central)
5. Singer Works
6. Milngavie or Springburn
7. Partick Hill or Charing Cross
8. Craigendoran or Shettleston
9. Hyndland depot
0. Queen Street
D. Dumbarton

Second Fig.   **Destination**
1. Fast via Anniesland
2. Fast via Jordanhill
3. Limited stop via Anniesland
4. Limited stop via Jordanhill
5. Stopping via Anniesland
6. Stopping via Jordanhill
7. Workers' train
9. Empty train

LONDON TRANSPORT EXECUTIVE HEADLAMP CODE

The same simple code of four or five aspects, which was introduced years ago, is still used, on L.T.E. trains. In recent months, however, the introduction of the L.T.E.'s train describing apparatus has rendered the old code obsolete and although it will continue to be used for some time yet, all new sets now being introduced have two lights only at front and rear, showing white and red respectively, and display no means of train identification.

METROPOLITAN AND DISTRICT

NOTE: Through shortage of space only one code can be illustrated in respect of each route listed in this section. It should be noted on 1947-59, 1938, surface and 1927, 1931 and 1935 District stock the lights will be seen grouped together below the right-hand window of the driver's cab as in the diagrams below. On "F", and some 1923 District stock, the lights are dispersed to the three corners of the front of the coach, as under, but the relative positions remain the same:—

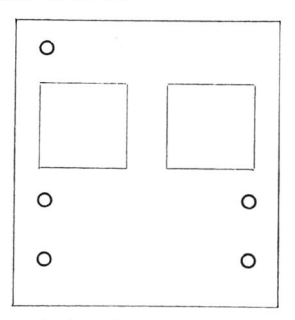

In the diagram below, hyphens denote lights not in use, and circles those which are illuminated to indicate the particular code

O O - O O	**UPMINSTER** (Eastbound) **HAMMERSMITH** (MET.) (Westbound)

O O O O O	**BARKING SIDINGS** (Both directions) **KENSINGTON** (Olympia)

O - O O O	**DAGENHAM** (Eastbound) **LIVERPOOL STREET** (Eastbound) **UXBRIDGE** (Westbound)

- O - O -	**WIMBLEDON** (Westbound)

- O - O O	**BARKING STATION** (Eastbound District) **PUTNEY BRIDGE** (Westbound)

O - - - O	**PLAISTOW** (Eastbound) **EALING BDY.** (Westbound) **KINGS CROSS** (Outer Rail*)

i.e., Clockwise round the Circle

Code	Station
- - - O O	**RICHMOND** (Westbound)
- O O O O	**KENSINGTON HIGH STREET** (Eastbound)
O - O O -	**WHITECHAPEL** (Both Directions)
- - O O O	**PARSONS GREEN** (Both Directions)
O O - - O	**MANSION HOUSE** (Eastbound) **WIMBLEDON** (from Edgware Road line†)
O - - O O	**ACTON TOWN** (Both Directions) **WEMBLEY PARK** (Both Directions)
O O - O -	**CHARING CROSS** (Eastbound) **NORTHFIELDS** (Westbound) **BARKING STATION** (Eastbound Metropolitan)
O - - O -	**HOUNSLOW W.** (Westbound)
- O - - O	**S. KENSINGTON** (Eastbound)
O O O O -	**EALING COMMON** (Both Directions)
- - - O -	**CIRCLE** (Both Directions or Both Rails)
O - - - -	**MOORGATE (MET.)** (Eastbound) To and from **RICKMANSWORTH***
- O O - O	**GLOUCESTER ROAD** (Both Directions)
O O O - O	**NEASDEN** (Both Directions)

* On southbound journey, code to be changed at Harrow-on-the-Hill according to destination
† Only trains non-stopping certain stations

Lights	Destination
`- / O O / O -`	**EARLS COURT** (Both Directions)
`O / - O / - O`	**EDGWARE ROAD** (Both Directions) **RAYNERS LANE** (Westbound)
`- / - / - O`	**HARROW-ON-THE-HILL** (Northbound) **BAKER STREET (MAIN)** (Southbound)
`- / - O / O -`	**ALDGATE** (Outer Rail)* **WATFORD (DIRECT)**† (Northbound)

METROPOLITAN COMPARTMENT STOCK AND ELECTRIC LOCOMOTIVES

NOTE: On this stock three light positions only are available, at top centre, on lower left and right of the cab front

Lights	Destination
`O / O -`	**ALDGATE** (Outer Rail)*
`O / O O`	**WEMBLEY PARK** (Both Directions)
`O / - O`	**LIVERPOOL STREET** (Outer Rail)* **UXBRIDGE** (Westbound)
`- / - O`	**HARROW-ON-THE-HILL** (Northbound) **BAKER STREET (MAIN)** (Southbound)
`. / O O`	**NEASDEN** (Both Directions)
`O / - -`	**MOORGATE (MET.)** (Eastbound) To and from **RICKMANSWORTH**§
`O / O -`	**WATFORD (DIRECT)** (Northbound) **WATFORD (Via N. Curve)**† (Northbound from Rickmansworth only)

* i.e., Clockwise round the Circle
† Northbound Watford trains via N. Curve carry Rickmansworth code to Rickmansworth, and change there to Watford (Direct) code
§ Southbound trains to change code to relevant destination at Harrow, or earlier if non-stopping

"F" STOCK ON E. LONDON LINE

▫ ‑ ▫ ‑ ‑ ‑ ○ ○ ▫	**NEW CROSS** (Southbound) **SHOREDITCH** (Northbound)

▫ ‑ ▫ ‑ ‑ ‑ ▫ ‑ ○	**NEW CROSS GATE** (Southbound)

▫ ‑ ▫ ‑ ‑ ‑ ○ ‑ ▫	**WHITECHAPEL** (E.L.) (Both Directions)

CENTRAL LINE

‑ ○ ‑ ○	**LOUGHTON & EPPING LINE** (Eastbound) **RUISLIP GARDENS** **W. RUISLIP** (Westbound)

‑ ○ ‑ ‑	**WHITE CITY** (Both Directions) **WOODFORD** (Both Directions)

‑ ○ ○ ‑	**GRANGE HILL** (Via WOODFORD) (Eastbound) **NORTHOLT** (Westbound)

‑ ○ ○ ○	**LEYTONSTONE** (Westbound)

‑ ‑ ○ ○	**NEWBURY PARK & HAINAULT LINE** (Eastbound) **EALING BDY.** (Westbound)

‑ ‑ ○ ‑	**WOODFORD‑HAINAULT** **LOUGHTON‑EPPING** **LIVERPOOL STREET‑MARBLE ARCH** **SHUTTLE SERVICES**

PICCADILLY LINE

- ○ - ○	**COCKFOSTERS** (Eastbound) **HOUNSLOW WEST** (Westbound)
- - ○ -	**ACTON TOWN** (Both Directions)
- ○ ○ -	**OAKWOOD** (Eastbound) **RAYNERS LANE** (Westbound)
- - - ○	**NORTHFIELDS** (Both Directions)
- - ○ ○	**ARNOS GROVE** (Eastbound) **SOUTH HARROW** (Westbound)
- ○ - -	**ALL OTHER DESTINATIONS**
- ○ ○ ○	**WOOD GREEN** (Eastbound) **UXBRIDGE** (Westbound)

NORTHERN LINE

○ ○ ○ ○ ○	**ALL DESTINATIONS**

BAKERLOO LINE

⠛	STANMORE	⠻	WEMBLEY PARK
⠱	NEASDEN	⠌	WATFORD JUNCTION
⠑	QUEENS PARK	⠊	ELEPHANT & CASTLE
⠰	HARROW & WEALDSTONE	⠪	LONDON ROAD DEPOT
⠆	EMPTY TRAINS HARROW & WEALDSTONE	⠬	EMPTY TRAINS CROXLEY SHED WATFORD JUNCTION